ENGLISH CASTLES

Warkworth Castle,
Northumberland.

ENGLISH
CASTLES

RICHARD HUMBLE

HARMONY BOOKS
NEW YORK

Dunstanburgh in Northumbria, subjected to 'ordeal by cannon' in the Wars of the Roses : a view of the outer Lilburn Tower from the gatehouse.

Endpapers : Rochester Castle, Kent

Published by Harmony Books, a division of Crown Publishers, Inc., One Park Avenue, New York, New York 10016.
HARMONY and colophon are trademarks of Crown Publishers, Inc.

Printed in Italy

Library of Congress Cataloging in Publication Data

Humble, Richard.
English castles.
Includes index.
1. Castles—England. I. Title.
NA7745.H85   1984   725'.18'0942   84-4534
ISBN 0-517-55410-0

10 9 8 7 6 5 4 3 2 1
First American Edition

CONTENTS

THE SOUTH-WEST

EAST ANGLIA

THE MIDLANDS

CONTENTS

Norham
Bamburgh
Dunstanburgh
Alnwick
Warkworth

Newcastle

Carlisle
Durham

Brougham
Barnard Castle
Brough
Richmond
Bolton
Scarborough
Helmsley
Pickering
York
Skipton

THE NORTH COUNTRY

Conisbrough

Peveril
Lincoln

Beeston
Newark
Tattershall

THE MIDLANDS

Castle
Rising
Caister
Norwich

Acton
Burnell
Bridgnorth
Ashby-de-la-Zouch

EAST ANGLIA

Stokesay
Dudley
Ludlow
Orford
Framlingham
Warwick

Castle
Hedingham

Goodrich
Colchester

Berkhamsted
Hadleigh

Berkeley
Windsor
London

Donnington
Upnor
Rochester

Farleigh
Hungerford
**THE
SOUTH COUNTRY**
Farnham
**THE
SOUTH-EAST**
Walmer
Deal

Nunney
Bodiam
Saltwood
Dover
Old Sarum
Arundel
Lewes

**THE
SOUTH-WEST**
Sherborne
Portchester
Pevensey

Okehampton
Christchurch
Hurst

Tintagel
Corfe
Carisbrooke
Berry
Launceston
Pomeroy
Yarmouth
Totnes
Restormel
Dartmouth
Pendennis
St Mawes

'THE BONES OF THE KINGDOM'

Author's note

All castles in this book are 'real' castles – that is, 'large fortified buildings or sets of buildings, strongholds' – and not, as the *Concise Oxford Dictionary* continues, 'mansions that were once such'. This excludes all great houses with 'castle' names like Castle Howard in Yorkshire, splendid neo-Victorian confections like Castle Drogo in Devon, or comparatively modern renovations like Hever Castle in Kent. (Readers interested in castles as stately residences rather than as fighting strongholds are recommended to Russell Chamberlin's *Great English Houses* in this series.)

Nor have I included much older fortifications from the Bronze and early Iron Ages, all of them undoubted strongholds, which also happen to be called castles. (The best-known of these and undoubtedly the most majestic is the gigantic triple ring of Maiden Castle in Dorset.) These great Celtic ring fortifications are nevertheless well worth visiting in their own right, and are comprehensively described by Richard Cavendish in *Prehistoric England*, also in this series.

Instruments of royal power

The first true castles in England were sited and built during and immediately after the Norman Conquest of 1066–72 – to hasten the defeat of the English population and keep it firmly under the control of the King and his trusted lieutenants, the new ruling caste. Royal control, direct or delegated, was the primary role of the castle in England; and this role never changed over the next six hundred years, even after the arrival of gunpowder and cannon. From the second half of the eleventh century to the first half of the seventeenth, castles remained both symbols and instruments of royal power in England, enabling that power to be exercised by force whenever necessary. This was why the victorious Parliamentarians, after beating King Charles I in the English Civil War of 1642–8, reduced to ruins (or 'slighted') all the major castles which had been held for the King during the fighting. The 'ruins that Cromwell knocked about a bit' were not created in blind revenge or unthinking vandalism, but as a deliberate attempt to destroy the provincial underpinning of royalist power in England.

Reduced to ruins after its long Civil War siege, Corfe Castle still dominates the natural gap through the Purbeck Hills in south-east Dorset.

A linear castle developed from a central motte-and-bailey: Arundel in Sussex, showing how the western curtain wall abuts with the keep on its motte.

Windsor, a close cousin to Arundel, but with the Round Tower on its motte completely enclosed by the curtain wall. St George's Chapel is on the left.

The republican victory of 1649 was short-lived: ten years of military dictatorship were more than enough to see the English welcoming Charles II home from exile in the summer of 1660. Nevertheless, the Civil War had accomplished a decisive and final shift of power from Crown to Parliament. After the Restoration, with Parliament holding the national purse strings, the castles of England could never return to their former status as the front-line bastions of royal power throughout the land. Nor were aristocratic families, returning to or taking over estates once governed from great castles, motivated to repair the ruins and restore every castle to its former glory. The taste was now for elegant and spacious mansions with the accent on grace and comfort rather than defence.

Stone and brick castles, however, were built to last, and it would have taken much longer than a couple of centuries of redundancy and neglect to wipe them off the English landscape. (Remember that Hadrian's Wall, the coast-to-coast northern frontier of the Roman Empire, survived nearly 1,500 years of being used as a convenient stone quarry, before archaeologists and preservationists began seriously trying to save what was left.) By the late eighteenth century castles were back in fashion – not so much for their historical interest, but as picturesque ornaments of the English landscape.

A new role: landscape ornaments

The eighteenth-century landscape gardeners, looking at the natural features of the land with a new eye, used castle ruins to enhance the beautiful gardens and estates being laid out as settings for the great houses of England's ruling class. This was a less ironical or ignominious fate than it seems. Every castle in the land had been deliberately sited to command the surrounding landscape, even though this had been done with military rather than aesthetic purposes in mind. The landscape gardeners of the eighteenth century were the first to exploit the fact that there is no such thing as a castle with a bad view – which makes castles so rewarding for visitors today.

Indeed, in the later eighteenth and nineteenth centuries the demand for castle ruins far outran supply of the genuine article, making this period the golden age for the construction of fake ruins, or follies. Theirs is a fascinating story in itself, but sadly follies, like mansions and Celtic hill-forts, fall outside the scope of this book.

This new appreciation of castles as 'landscape improvers' was assisted by prodigious changes in the landscape itself, wrought in the same period by England's Agricultural Revolution. By the end of the eighteenth century thousands of square miles of new farming land had been brought under cultivation, stripped of the forests which had carpeted England practically from sea to sea as little as two hundred years before. Further acreage had been won by the taming of waste land and the draining of marshes. This tidying-up of the English countryside, which by the 1870s resulted in England being the most efficient farming nation in the world, helped invest the castles of England with a natural prominence in the landscape which had never before been so marked.

The Victorian achievement

All this went hand in glove with the nineteenth-century 'Gothic Revival' of interest in the Middle Ages, with best-selling novels like Sir Walter Scott's *Ivanhoe* boosting popular interest in castles and their past. It helped make the nineteenth and early twentieth centuries the last great period of castle-building in England. Business fortunes made in commerce and industry were translated into mock medieval castles, often complete with drawbridge or portcullis. In these replica castles, Victorian tastes were furnished in Gothic flamboyance, with results ranging from the beautiful to the cheerfully appalling. In general it is fair to say that Victorian neo-medieval architects achieved far less dire results with castles than they did with ancient churches or university buildings. (At Oxford the new-look Balliol College, apparently modelled on the imposing railway terminus buildings appearing in the cities, attracted the deathless comment 'C'est magnifique, mais ce n'est pas la gare.') Two outstanding examples of nineteenth-century renovation work on famous medieval castles are included in these pages: **Arundel** (p. 42) and **Windsor** (p. 48).

To this enthusiastic fostering of interest in England's medieval buildings, the Victorians added a transport revolution spanning the length and breadth of the land. Travel by rail, with over 20,000 miles of railway completed by 1890, was made possible by the most comprehensive public transport network ever seen in England (or ever likely to be). The expansion of the railways left no spot in Britain more than an hour's journey from a railway station. Cheap and easy excursion travel by rail created a domestic tourist industry which expanded out of all measure after the advent of the motor car and family touring by road. And castles have always ranked among the most popular assets of England's tourist industry.

Visiting castles

One very good reason why castles are such marvellous places to visit is because, as mentioned above, there is no such thing as a castle with a bad view; building a castle without an all-round panorama of the surrounding countryside would have been as pointless as building an underground lighthouse. Then there is the variety. No two English castles are the same – not even 'series castles' built in the same period and to the same basic specifications, like Henry VIII's south coastal chain from Deal to Pendennis. In each case, the demands of the site and the availability of materials produced a building with its own unique combination of features. Castles *had* to be different one from the other, to make them as hard as possible to capture: one of the most important functions of the castle was to present attackers with a unique set of problems to which there was no stock solution.

Castles were blatant statements of the owners' worldly wealth and power. They were places where laws were enforced and punishment dealt out, often in hideous measure; where men trained for war and, not infrequently, fought, and were killed or horribly wounded. They were also places of squalor and disease, especially when resisting long sieges. But this is only part of the story: castles were also places where people of both high and low social status

From the later fourteenth century, 'keyhole' gunports were built into town walls and new castles such as Bodiam in order to deter attackers.

11

The imposing Newel Staircase at Tattershall in Lincolnshire. Broad glazed windows show the fifteenth-century accent on domestic comfort.

played sports, feasted, made music, and lived life to the full.

An enduring test of great architecture is that neither human destructiveness nor the passing of the centuries manage to dispel the original purpose of the builders. Ruined abbeys like Glastonbury, Tintern or Fountains remain cloaked in reverence, but with castles – even brutally blitzed specimens like **Corfe** (p. 60) – it is the worldliness which has survived. Where churches exist to funnel one's imagination towards God and the next life, castles let the imagination run riot about the mundane details of living in former ages. All this can make castles a lot more fun to visit.

Far more often than not, a castle visit involves a good deal of clambering about, in or on mysterious and exciting ruins, and children particularly love spiral staircases up towers pierced with firing-slits. Tell them to watch out for spiral stairs which turn to the right. These were specially designed to favour defenders beating a fighting retreat to the upper levels. The right-hand turn obliged attackers to fight their way up with their sword arms uncomfortably close to the central spine of the staircase, while the defenders were left with plenty of room for

downward cutting and thrusting. Once up, and making the round of the battlements or enjoying the view from the top of a tower keep, visitors are automatically cast in the role of sentries on watch; but this was also where the castle's upper crust would come to enjoy a breath of fresh air and a gentle stroll, well above the bustle and smells at ground level.

If the castle has a Great Hall with walls still standing, look for the rows of sockets which held the

One of the earliest castle amenities: outfalls for garderobes (latrines), built into the castle's outer wall above the ditch or moat.

cross-beams of upper floors and galleries. Before you leave the hall, notice the distance from the kitchens and wonder if cooked food ever arrived still hot on the tables in the hall.

As for that classic castle feature, the dungeon, bear in mind that not every underground chamber was necessarily a prison or torture-chamber. During a siege the safest place for women, children and wounded was underground. And large underground store-rooms were often built to take inflammable items, such as firewood, which could not be left lying around in the open where enemy fire-missiles could set them ablaze. On the ground and upper levels, if you find what looks like a one-man cell built into the wall with no exit but a downward drain, it was probably a simple *garderobe* ('protect-your-clothes') or latrine, sluiced out with the occasional bucket of water when it became too ripe.

This book is intended to whet the appetite for castle-visiting in England by providing nationwide coverage of the entire range of castle types open to the public. The best individual castle histories and architectural descriptions are to be found in the excellent booklets on sale at castles in the care of the Department of the Environment, the National Trust or private ownership. But when visiting castles for the first time, a certain amount of general knowledge about castles and their time is most useful. The following information will help visitors to recognize basic castle types and layouts.

MOTTE-AND-BAILEY

The first castles (c. 1066–1189)
Norman kings: William I (1066–87), William II (1087–1100), Henry I (1100–35),
Stephen (1135–54); Henry II, first Angevin king (1154–89)

Founded, according to tradition, in 911, the Duchy of Normandy was the first European society since the Roman Empire to perfect the regular use of fortifications in war. The Normans used their *castella*, from which the word 'castle' derives, to guarantee the security of base areas and to dominate newly-won territory. By about 1050, the Normans had developed an 'instant' castle which could be built at great speed using local peasant labour and timber. This consisted of a mound of earth thrown up from a circular ditch, with the top ringed by a wooden stockade and a two- or three-storey wooden tower (*donjon*) in the middle. This mound, usually about 50 feet (15 m) high, was called the *motte*, and it was encircled at ground level by another ditch and stockade enclosing an outer defensive area known as a *bailey*. Where the size of the castle and the lie of the land permitted, additional security would be provided by adding a second or outer bailey. All surrounding trees and undergrowth outside the outer bailey stockade would then be swept away to leave an unimpeded all-round view from the castle, making surprise attacks impossible.

These castles were carefully sited to command key roads, river crossings and strategic high ground. The better chosen the castle site, the more dangerous it was for an enemy force to ignore the castle and bypass it, for this was an invitation to the castle garrison to sally out and attack the enemy's communications. The castle's prime role was to deny the enemy freedom of movement: to force him to sit down for a siege instead of moving on to achieve his true objective.

How long a motte-and-bailey castle could hold out depended on two factors: the size of the garrison and of its stock of provisions, and how much the attackers knew about reducing castles. The latter proved the decisive factor in Norman-occupied England, where castles on the Norman model were a frightening novelty. Vivid scenes in the earlier sections of the Bayeux Tapestry show professionals at work: Duke William's knights attacking Dol and Dinan Castles in Brittany. Even allowing for artist's licence, it is clear that the trick was to start by overrunning the bailey, forcing the garrison to retreat up the wooden ramp leading from the bailey to the motte. (Attacking the motte first would enable the garrison to counter-attack from the bailey.) Once the garrison was safely holed up inside the motte defences, its attention was fixed by feint attacks up the ramp while flanking parties crept forward to fire the motte's stockade, leaving the garrison with no option but surrender.

Fire was always the greatest enemy of these 'first-generation' wooden castles, but the beauty of the

A classic example of the Norman motte-and-bailey: Pleshey Castle in Essex, which never made the twelfth-century transition to stone defences.

system was that the motte-and-bailey foundation site, once created, could not be so easily destroyed. It was an easy job to recommission a burned-out castle by building new wooden defences. William I's first motte-and-bailey castle at York, built in 1068, was burned out in the Northern Rising of September 1069 but rebuilt before the end of the year; and **Clifford's Tower** (p. 124) still squats on the original Norman motte thrown up 915 years ago. The confusion of the defeated English is reflected by

How to attack a motte-and-bailey, from the Bayeux Tapestry: Duke William's men are shown firing the keep palisade of Dinan Castle in Brittany.

the familiar words 'dungeon' and 'moat', with their accepted meanings of underground chamber and water-filled ditch – both of which are about as far from the original *donjon* and *motte* as it is possible to get.

The earliest picture of a motte-and-bailey castle being built in England is in the Bayeux Tapestry: the construction of the castle at Hastings, built to protect Duke William's base camp after his army landed at Pevensey on 28 September 1066. The tapestry shows a working party of peasants with

The earliest contemporary picture of Norman stone defences on a motte: Duke William's castle at Bayeux, with William shown arriving at centre.

mattocks and shovels, closely supervised by armed Normans. The labourers are shovelling stones and soil to build up the motte which, unlike other, older castles shown in the tapestry, is layered. This is presumably a deliberate reference to the alternating layers of gravel and rammed earth of the motte's core. Wherever possible, Norman engineers would site a castle where a natural hillock or knoll offered a solid foundation for the motte, because it took decades for the mounded earth to settle. Medieval records from all over England are packed with references to castle damage caused by soil subsidence, usually with the motte as main culprit.

The motte-and-bailey castle remained the basic 'instant' castle type long after the Norman Conquest, well into the latter years of the twelfth

The Bayeux Tapestry depicts the building of the first Norman motte-and-bailey on English soil: Hastings, built to protect the Norman beach-head.

century. As well as serving as a strategic weapon during campaigns of conquest and retribution, the castle was the focal point of royal power as delegated to the king's vassals on their estates, or manors. When effective royal rule broke down, as during the 'Anarchy' in the mid-twelfth century under King Stephen, the result would be an epidemic of castle-building, as petty lords kicked over the traces and strengthened their local power-bases in the shires. One of the first tasks confronting the tough young Henry II when he succeeded Stephen in 1154 was to bring his vassals to heel, destroying these unauthorized or 'adulterine' castles by the score. This is one reason why there are hundreds of motte-and-bailey sites across mainland Britain, and also in Ireland, the invasion of which was launched under Henry II in 1170. Most of these sites are now overgrown and recognizable only by the grassy hump of the motte – the stamp of the Norman conqueror and his heirs.

England's most sophisticated shell keep: Clifford's Tower at York. Its graceful outline is created by four interlocking circular towers.

The transition to stone: shell keeps

Clifford's Tower at York (p. 124), **Arundel** (p. 42), **Windsor** (p. 48), and **Pickering** (p. 123) are perfect examples of how an original motte-and-bailey site formed the core of later and much more elaborate stone-built castles. In all cases this expansion began with the fireproofing of first gener-

ation motte-and-bailey castles, with stone *curtain walls* replacing the original bailey stockades and a circular *shell keep* instead of the wooden donjon tower on top of the motte.

But it is at smaller castles, of less strategic importance or where the lie of the land forbade such expansion, that the original motte-and-bailey format can best be appreciated. **Totnes** (p. 69), **Launceston** (p. 78) and **Restormel** (p. 71) all lie tucked away in the South-West, far from the military frontiers with Wales and Scotland where castle expansion and strengthening was most naturally favoured. All three are shell keeps, or motte-and-bailey castles rebuilt in stone in the twelfth and early thirteenth centuries: fossil specimens, as it were, of England's first castles.

The first stone castles:
tower keeps
(c. 1080–1189)

Although the ubiquitous motte-and-bailey was the basic 'front-line' castle of the Norman Conquest and its aftermath, the Normans never relied on it exclusively. While it was easy to build and repair, the motte-and-bailey was also much too vulnerable to fire (both accidental and deliberate), and too small for much more than the most immediate needs of local defence. By the end of William I's reign, therefore, the most important of the king's stone strongholds were being constructed on an entirely different plan. These were the massive, multi-storey *tower keeps*, screened from direct assault by baileys and later enclosed by more elaborate stone defence-works. The classic eleventh-century tower keeps are the Conqueror's **White Tower** at London (p. 26) and the keep at **Colchester** (p. 82), followed by the twelfth-century tower keeps at **Rochester** (p. 34) and **Dover** (p. 32).

The Norman tower keep is the ultimate statement of the Conquest: brute force come to stay. This, one feels, is what the *Anglo-Saxon Chronicle* had in mind with its bitter verse epitaph of William I, which begins 'He had castles built, and poor men stark oppressed'. These tower keeps are sheer, two- to three-storey blocks of masonry, impossible to contemplate at close quarters without a catch of the breath; even the very best photographs rarely capture their brooding menace. The walls are 90–100 feet high (27·5–30·5 m) and enormously thick – 15 feet (4·6 m) in the White Tower, 21 feet (6·4 m) at Dover. For additional strength their lower levels were packed with earth, with an outside staircase flush with the wall leading to a single entrance on the first storey. This would be closed for defence with a massive wooden door, most probably two-ply, with the grain of the two layers running at right-angles to each other to create an axe-proof slab. The quickest way through this would be a fire started with

brushwood bundles and buckets of pitch – which the defenders would naturally attempt to put out with water dumped from the battlement and upper storeys.

The net result was a murderous bottleneck which attackers had to attempt to pierce under a hail of missiles from the battlement, the upper storeys, and the flat-sided turrets jutting out from the corners of the keep. Any attacking force which did manage to burn down the door and force its way into the first storey immediately came up against a mighty cross-wall dividing the keep's interior in two, leaving all the work of breaking and entering to be done again; and again on the upper storeys, assuming that the decimated attackers had not already been wiped out or forced to retreat by a counter-attack.

Brutally effective against frontal attack, the tower keep achieved economy in defence by forcing attackers to expose themselves to concentrated fire-power at a single point. But the tower keep had four great weaknesses: its corners, which were always vulnerable to the tactic of mining. Drive a long tunnel under one of the keep's corners, pack the end with wood and set it ablaze, and the resulting cave-in would bring the rubble-packed masonry above down with a run, creating a gaping breach.

This happened at Rochester in the winter of 1215, when King John besieged a rebel garrison in the castle. After a two-month siege the keep was still holding out long after the bailey defences had been overrun, and John ordered his miners into action. The King's famous choice of fuel for the completed mine consisted of 40 bacon pigs 'of the sort least good for eating'. The blazing bacon fat did the trick and Rochester's south-east corner turret collapsed in ruin – but even then the defenders did not give up. Alerted to what was coming, probably by the usual mine-detecting method (bowls of water whose surface would tremble from the shock-waves of the miners' picks), the garrison had pulled back beyond the internal cross-wall of the keep, and fought on. But the defenders were now cut off from their last food stocks, and only a few days were needed for the work of the slowest, surest siege weapon of all – hunger – to compel their surrender.

The Rochester siege of 1215 is a perfect demonstration of the strengths and weaknesses of the tower keep. When Rochester's ruined corner tower was rebuilt, it was in the much stronger rounded cross-section which became the hallmark of castle-building in the thirteenth and fourteenth centuries.

The soaring mass of the immense tower keep at Rochester in Kent, built in the early twelfth century as a bishop's palace as well as a stronghold.

'Hermit-crab' castles (c. 1070–1154)

In addition to motte-and-bailey castles and tower keeps, the Normans were never slow to plant castles on sites where there were existing defence-works, dating back to Roman times and before. These may be thought of as 'hermit-crab' castles, where the genius of Norman castle-building took over the abandoned shells of ancient strongholds and gave them a new lease of life. Three fine examples of these 'hermit-crab' castles are **Old Sarum** (p. 55), **Pevensey** (p. 38) and **Portchester** (p. 52).

Old Sarum was where William I disbanded his army in 1070, after his terrible punitive campaign against the Northern rebels which left Yorkshire a blackened desert. In the centre of the circular Celtic earthwork and ditch a second ring was dug and a motte raised in the middle: a circular 'bullseye' motte-and-bailey, converted to a stone castle in the reign of Henry I. The Celtic outer ring was renovated to shelter a cathedral town (the site of the cathedral can also be inspected when visiting this fine castle). But this arrangement did not prove successful; the churchmen objected to living under the constant military jurisdiction of the castle, and a new cathedral was founded on the site of modern Salisbury, 1½ miles (2·4 km) south of Old Sarum castle, in 1220.

Pevensey and Portchester, however, were girdled with the mighty stone ramparts characteristic of the coastal fortresses built by the Romans to defend the 'Saxon Shore' against Saxon raids in the fourth century AD. These fortresses consisted of huge curtain walls studded with rounded projecting bastions. At both sites, the Normans built a tower keep at one corner of the Roman walls, cutting off part of the enclosed space to form an inner bailey. Similar work was begun at a third 'Saxon Shore' fortress in Suffolk: Burgh Castle, 2 miles (3·2 km) west of modern Yarmouth on the Waveney river. At Burgh a motte and bailey were sited at the south-east corner of the Roman perimeter, but here the transition to stone was never achieved. When a castle was eventually completed in the area it was at **Caister**, 4 miles (6·5 km) north of Burgh, in the early fifteenth century. Visitors to Caister (p. 93) should try to find time for a quick look at Burgh, a good example of a Norman castle 'graft' which did not take.

THE GREAT YEARS OF CASTLE BUILDING

Linear and concentric castles (c. 1189–1377)
Angevin kings: Richard I (1189–99), John (1199–1216); Plantagenet kings: Henry III (1216–72),
Edward I (1272–1307), Edward II (1307–27) and Edward III (1327–77)

The period from the mid-twelfth to the mid-thirteenth centuries was a 'melting-pot' century in English castle development, prompted by a flood of new ideas on castle defences from the Continent and, thanks to the Crusades, from the Middle East. They added up to the removal of obvious weak spots in the defence system by strengthening the main gate and the outer curtain wall. The latter was also extended, so that the keep was now surrounded by outer defences instead of merely being the strongest point of the perimeter.

After the tower keeps of the first century of castle-building came the tower gatehouse, developed as the strongest sector of the curtain wall – and invariably, if the castle did not have an earlier keep, the strongest part of the whole castle. 'Murder holes', in the ceiling of the gatehouse porch through which all the castle's traffic passed, enabled rocks, red-hot irons and showers of red-hot sand to be rained down on any attackers foolhardy enough to try to break through. Curtain walls were extended and rebuilt with projecting towers from which attackers, no matter from which direction they tried to approach, would be caught in a crossfire from the walls. And, wherever feasible, water-filled moats were added as the most effective answer to mining.

Step by step, all these improvements led steadily towards the great concentric and linear castles of the late thirteenth century, in which outer and inner defences formed an integrated whole and the original function of a central keep became redundant. A remarkably early specimen of these 'keepless' castles is **Framlingham** in Suffolk (p. 86), built between 1178 and 1213. Here all the eggs were put in one basket: a gigantic curtain wall studded with thirteen rectangular flanking towers, and no keep.

Yet Framlingham was the exception which proved the rule; in general the tower keep, either free-standing or spliced into an angle of the curtain wall, remained a favourite standby of English castle-building until the early fifteenth century. Few other basic elements of castle architecture underwent so many drastic changes, all aimed at improving strength and habitability. **Orford** tower keep (p. 85), is another startling East Anglian novelty dating from the second half of the twelfth century. There is little to indicate that Orford was built in the same period, and to the orders of the same king (Henry II) as the massive rectangular keep at Dover. Orford was actually completed in 1173, over ten years *before* Dover; yet the two are as different as chalk from cheese. The Orford keep is polygonal

Framlingham in Suffolk, perhaps the most impressive early attempt at a 'keepless' castle, with thirteen rectangular towers studding the curtain wall.

Strengthening the tower keep : Conisbrough, South Yorkshire, with six flanking towers rising from a battered or inward-sloping base.

outside, cylindrical inside, and braced by three rectangular flanking towers: a handsome blend of elegance and strength. Nor is Orford an isolated one-off design, like Framlingham. There is a similar tower keep at **Conisbrough** in Yorkshire (p. 116), cylindrical with *six* rectangular flanking towers, and smaller polygonal keeps are to be found at Chilham in Kent, Odiham in Hampshire and Tickhill in Yorkshire.

The next logical step after polygonal and cylindrical tower keeps braced with external flanking towers was the fully cylindrical keep. This offered the best all-round streamlining against battering with rocks by siege artillery, and presented the strongest cross-section to mining operations. Yet the *round keep*, as distinct from the shell keep, is the greatest rarity of all in English castles (there are seven in Wales: Bronllys and Tretower in Breconshire, Dynevor in Carmarthenshire, Dolbadarn in Caernarvonshire, Pembroke, and Caldicot and Skenfrith in Monmouthshire). The best surviving example is at **Launceston** in Cornwall (p. 78), where a round keep was built inside the shell keep. England has nothing like the huge cylindrical tower keep of Richard I's Château Gaillard, built in 1197–8 to keep the French out of Normandy, which resembles nothing so much as a Saturn I rocket in stone. The reason for this is that by the middle thirteenth century, when the cylindrical keep might have been expected to be the latest trend, English castle design was already drifting faster and faster towards the symmetrical, concentric and linear types which either enclosed existing keeps, or rendered the building of new ones unnecessary.

The finest examples of concentric castle-building in Britain fall outside the scope of this book. They are the graceful giants built to the orders of Edward I (1272–1307) to keep the conquered Welsh under the English thumb – Caernarvon, Conway, Beaumaris and Harlech. But the preparatory work for these magnificent achievements in stone – all of which were designed and built 'in one' – had been done in England. The English prototype for the great Edwardian concentric castles, in which the baileys (or *wards*) enclose each other, was achieved with the expansion of the Tower of London in the reign of Henry III (1216–72). Henry's son, Edward I, completed the job by adding the Tower's outer curtain wall and flanking towers. Another superb conversion dating from Edward I's reign is **Goodrich** in Hereford and Worcester (p. 98), where the

The twelfth-century tower keep of Goodrich (Hereford and Worcester), enclosed by later curtain defences to create a powerful concentric castle complex.

curtain wall and towers enclose a late twelfth-century square keep.

But the idea of adding full circuits of curtain walls and towers was also applied to castles sited for the domination of high ground or ridges, where big contour changes made concentric designs impossible. The result here was the linear castle, best typified by **Windsor** (p. 48) and **Arundel** (p. 42), where the wards are enclosed in a chain instead of one inside the other. Linear defences were also adopted at **Warkworth** (p. 144), dominated by an imposing cruciform stone tower built on the original motte in the fourteenth century.

It was in these years that the fortified outwork known as the *barbican* was introduced. At its best, the barbican, which always blocked the approach to the main gatehouse, was a 'mini-castle' pushed forward from the outer castle defences. Sometimes this was extended to provide not double but triple security from surprise attack. At London the barbican (the now-vanished Lion Tower) covered the twin outer defences of the Middle Tower, which in turn covered the main landward entrance through Edward I's outer curtain: the Byward Tower. At **Pickering** (p. 123) the entire southern or Outer Ward served as a barbican, screening the main castle defences. Other barbican defences of differing types, all best contrived to suit the needs of the site and of the existing defences of the time, can be seen at **Donnington** (p. 46), **Dunstanburgh** (p. 142), **Helmsley** (p. 126), **Richmond** (p. 118) and **Scarborough** (p. 120).

FROM CASTLES TO FORTIFIED HOUSES

(c. 1350–1485)
Plantagenet kings: Edward III (1327–77), Richard II (1377–99);
Lancastrian kings: Henry IV (1399–1413), Henry V (1413–22),
Henry VI (1422–61); Yorkist kings: Edward IV (1461–83), Richard III (1483–5)

All these far-reaching improvements to castle defences may be said to have reached their peak by the middle of the fourteenth century, and they carried English medieval castle-building to its zenith of effectiveness. The last of the great Plantagenet castle-builders was Edward III, who showed all his grandfather's flair and more. Sadly, Edward III's superb castle at Queenborough on the Isle of Sheppey no longer exists; but its foundations have been excavated, proving it to have been beyond doubt the most powerful and sophisticated concentric castle ever built on English soil.

Built in 1361, Queenborough was circular: a ring of curtain wall unadorned with towers, save at the main gatehouse on the western side, which was flanked by twin towers. Queenborough's circular core was guarded by six towers, with the only way in through a second gatehouse halfway round the circle from the first. Cross-walls divided the inner defences into nine separate compartments, each intended to support its neighbours. The innermost circle was left clear, enabling garrison troops to shift easily to the most endangered sector. That vital amenity of any castle, the well, was plumb in the middle. Parallel walls inside the first gatehouse and outside the second, connecting the outer and inner curtains, left attackers with no freedom of movement at all. At Queenborough, therefore, the concentric castle reached its ultimate form: a perfect killing-bottle for intruders.

By the late fourteenth century, the defences of castles like Queenborough had become so strong that sieges aimed at rapid capture – commonplace throughout the late eleventh, twelfth and early thirteenth centuries – had become largely a waste of effort. But this did not mean that castle development came to an abrupt halt. Mere defensibility against attack had long ceased to be the castle's only reason for existence. They were no longer merely local fortresses for the king and his barons, 'the bones of the kingdom', as the chronicler William of New-burgh had called them back in the eleventh century. Improved habitability had always gone hand in

The dream castle – Bodiam in East Sussex, built under royal licence in the later fourteenth century. The wide moat kept enemy cannon at maximum range.

hand with improved defensibility; as residences of the country's royalty and aristocracy, castles were focal points of society. In other words, English medieval castles were bound to reflect any important changes in English medieval society, and between the accession of Edward III in 1327 and the defeat and death of Richard III in 1485, English society underwent more change than at any time since the Norman Conquest.

The Conqueror's system had been based on land tenure by the provision of military service on demand, with a peasantry fettered by bondage at the bottom of the feudal pyramid. But as the king's government moved away from purely military concerns and took on the functions of a civil government it needed annual injections of tax money drawn from all over the country. In less than a generation after the Conquest, cash rents had begun to replace military service, and by the second half of the fourteenth century this process had broken through to the bottom layer of the pyramid. The

Fireplaces and large windows for domestic comfort, built into the strong fifteenth-century tower of Ashby-de-la-Zouch in Leicestershire.

direct cause was a series of plague epidemics (not limited to the appalling 'Black Death' visitation in 1348–9) which reduced the population by nearly 30 per cent, causing an instant, nationwide labour shortage. For the first time ever, peasant labourers were in a position to push a series of runaway wage demands. But as wages soared, so did taxation (to pay for the wars in France), with the inevitable backlash of resentment against grasping landlords and Crown officials.

There is no space here to describe the resultant Peasants' Revolt of 1381, when the labourers of Kent and Essex marched on London to demand justice against their oppressors from the young King Richard II. Suffice it to say that the great royal castles of **Colchester, Rochester** and the **Tower of London** itself proved utterly useless as bastions against the Revolt. Garrisons which would probably have held out bravely against foreign invaders surrendered without a fight rather than be lynched by their own countrymen, and it will never be known for certain how much subversion and fifth-column work was involved. And the lesson was not forgotten. Though the Peasants' Revolt was the closest England came to the mass peasant risings (*Jacqueries*) suffered by France, the fear of repeated outbreaks inevitably left its mark on the ensuing century of castle-building in England.

The trauma of the Revolt confirmed a long-standing tendency of lords to fortify their manor houses against the possibility of local disturbances, making the late fourteenth and fifteenth centuries the heyday of the *domus defensabilis* or 'defensible home'. Because the need for security never eclipsed the need for more domestic comfort and grandeur, perhaps a better translation would be 'fortified stately home'. As with larger castles, these fortified manor houses consist of two basic types: those whose development spanned hundreds of years, and those (usually of the fifteenth or early sixteenth century) which were built in one go. Two fine examples of the former are **Ashby-de-la-Zouch** (p. 103) and **Stokesay** (p. 108). Perhaps the most impressive example of a fifteenth-century fortified manor, prompting the instinctive reaction 'Now that's what I *call* a castle!', is the massive brick tower of **Tattershall** (p. 101).

Castles and the coming of cannon

One of the greatest myths about castles is that the advent of gunpowder and cannon rendered them obsolete virtually overnight. This was true enough in the case of walled towns, but in general castles remained remarkably cannon-proof until, in the sixteenth and seventeenth centuries, the art of casting reliable heavy cannon was perfected. (Even with the high-velocity artillery of the Second World War, it was found that medieval fortifications needed a surprising amount of battering before they cracked.) When cannon arrived in the fourteenth century, castles adapted to this new military development, as they had always done. With its curtain wall and round corner towers, **Bodiam** in Sussex (p. 40) looks like a miniature concentric castle of the late thirteenth century. In fact it is a fortified manor house, built by licence of Richard II in 1385 – complete with 'keyhole' firing ports for cannon.

The first real test of cannon against castles came in the Wars of the Roses, fought intermittently between the factions of York and Lancaster between 1455 and 1485. About the only generalization which can be made about this confused conflict is that when castles fell to besiegers equipped with cannon – as did **Bamburgh** (p. 138) and the **Tower of London** (p. 26), to take just two examples – it was rarely due solely to the destructiveness of the artillery. The old factors of siege warfare still applied: the readiness of the defences, the extent of provision stockpiles, the likelihood of relief – not to

Majesty in brick: the splendid tower of Tattershall in Lincolnshire – like Bodiam in Sussex, restored by the munificence and dedication of Lord Curzon.

mention the chance of the garrison commander trying to save his neck by a timely surrender and quick change of sides – all added up to the state of the garrison's morale. The campaigns of the Wars of the Roses were nearly all settled by decisive field actions, such as St Albans, Northampton or Towton. At no stage was the result of such a battle reversed or even cancelled by an ensuing siege, with or without cannon.

This was particularly true of Henry Tudor's all-or-nothing march to victory on Bosworth Field in 1485 – a campaign in which castles and sieges played no part. It could be said that Bosworth, the last battle of the Wars of the Roses, symbolized the conflict as a whole. It was ultimately decided by which leading families, all with castles as their home bases, supported which claimant to the throne. The Wars of the Roses did *not* prove the obsolescence of castles in general – only of castles which were not, or could not be, equipped to reply to cannon with cannon.

THE TUDOR CASTLES

Platforms for geometric fire-power
Henry VIII (1509–47), Edward VI (1547–53),
Mary (1553–8), Elizabeth I (1558–1603)

The sixteenth century saw the last phase of royal castle-building in England, and in many ways it was the most extraordinary of them all. It certainly entitles Henry VIII to be ranked with his most famous castle-building forebears: Edward I, Henry II and William I. Henry's castles formed the most comprehensive system of coastal defence created since the Roman 'Saxon Shore' forts some 1,200 years earlier. Like his flagship, the recently recovered *Mary Rose* with its mixed armament of longbows and heavy guns, the castles of Henry VIII were a perfect synthesis of medieval and modern principles, tailored to the age of the cannon.

With the exception of the square block and straight-sided bastion of Yarmouth on the Isle of Wight, Henry VIII's castles were of circular or 'clover-leaf' (overlapping circles) design. Both of the two soundest late medieval principles were incorporated: a single gateway commanded by 'murder-holes' and a concentric layout, with outer and inner defences separated by a ditch or passage, itself commanded from both sides by walls loopholed for archery or musketry. The castle walls were squat and solid, presenting no easy target to enemy gunners, while covering every line of fire.

These castles were built to defend all vital anchorages of the King's other new creation: the Fleet, of which *Mary Rose* is the unique memorial. **Deal** (p. 30) and **Walmer** (p. 35) were sited to cover the anchorage of the Downs between the mainland and the Goodwin Sands. The main envisaged enemy was France, in alliance with the Holy Roman Empire. Henry's fears of a French attack were proved to be well founded by the French landing on the Isle of Wight in 1545 – the occasion of the tragic loss of *Mary Rose* – after which **Yarmouth** (p. 58) was built. In the South-West, the entrance to Falmouth Bay was covered from either side by **Pendennis** (p. 72) and **St Mawes** (p. 74).

These are the finest surviving examples of Henry VIII's castles, but they were by no means the only ones he built. There were five others at the Thames narrows of Tilbury and Gravesend, none of which have survived. And, like all great castle-builders, Henry VIII improved on the old as well as creating the new. He added three bastions to the outer defences at Dover, one of which (Moates Bulwark) still jabs like a defiant spear-head towards the line of attack from inland. And at London he added two massive semicircular bastions (Legge's Mount and the Brass Mount) to the northern angles of the Tower's outer curtain wall.

Under Elizabeth I (1558–1603), with the threat of Spanish instead of French invasion, there was widespread extending of castle fire-power by the addition of outer earthworks and bastions for the mounting of guns. One new Elizabethan castle, however, was **Upnor** (p. 36), built on the Medway to protect the Fleet base at Chatham.

The Civil War and after: an enduring legacy

The last fighting chapter in the story of England's castles was written in the English Civil War (1642–9), which saw more castles besieged in seven years than during the entire thirty years of the Wars of the Roses. These sieges are the best witness to the versatility of the castle over the centuries; it is remarkable how many Civil War sieges were conducted not against castles of the latest (Tudor) type, but against castles with pedigrees going right back to Norman motte-and-bailey days, like **Arundel**. The record was held by **Corfe**, stoutly defended for King Charles by the indomitable Lady Bankes from August 1644 to February 1646. Even then Corfe was not taken by direct attack, but by a fifth column of Parliamentarian troops admitted during fake negotiations. Corfe had been a famous Saxon royal residence a hundred years before the Norman Conquest – one of the very oldest 'bones of the kingdom'.

The active life of the castles certainly did not end with the Civil War. Henry VIII's castles were overhauled during the Napoleonic Wars, both for coastal defence and for the accommodation of French prisoners. The last bastion defence was hastily added to the Tower of London to keep out Chartist rioters in the early years of Queen

Tudor gun platform: Henry VIII's 'cloverleaf' castle at Deal in Kent, built low in a deep moat to command the Fleet anchorage of the Downs.

Victoria's reign; it was somewhat pointedly demolished by a German bomb in October 1940, and not replaced. This was the year before Hitler's Deputy, Rudolf Hess, was imprisoned in the Tower. In May 1940 the 'Miracle of Dunkirk' was improvised from Admiral Ramsay's HQ in **Dover Castle**, while inside the ancient Roman defences of **Pevensey**, machine-gun nests were cunningly constructed against the expected German invasion. Until the liberation of France four years later, Dover remained within range of German heavy guns – still the 'front door of England', as it had been 720 years before, when defended by Hubert de Burgh against French invaders and quisling barons.

THE SOUTH-EAST

THE TOWER OF LONDON

Department of the Environment
BR Fenchurch Street Station/4 mins walk;
BR Liverpool Street Station/78 bus; BR London Bridge
Station/47 bus to Tower Bridge Road/6 mins walk *or* 42 *or* 78 bus;
Green Line Coach to Minories Coach Station;
LT Underground, Circle or District Line, to Tower Hill Station

A casual visit to the Tower (say two hours or less) is really a waste of time and money; a day is hardly enough to do justice to its many attractions, any one of which – the Crown Jewels, the Armouries, St John's Chapel, the Royal Fusiliers Museum, the Changing of the Guard – would be well worth a visit on its own. Here we are concerned only with the Tower as a *castle*, and a unique specimen it is: the biggest, most complete concentric castle in all England, with William the Conqueror's White Tower at its core.

Visitors normally approach the Tower on foot, walking south from Tower Hill, with a good view of the green sweep of the dry Moat bed on the left, Edward I's outer curtain wall with Henry III's curtain wall beyond (both thirteenth-century), and

The Tower of London from the south, looking across the Thames from Tower Bridge, with Traitor's Gate and Bloody Tower to the left.

the pinnacles of the eleventh-century White Tower rising in the centre. One glance is enough to grasp the function of the concentric castle: successive belts of defence, getting tougher all the way in. As with nearly every English castle, the first mental exercise is to imagine the daunting effect of those cliffs of stone without the trees, none of which would have been permitted to grow in medieval times.

When passing through the Ticket Office, try to imagine the drawbridge which led into the Tower's now-vanished barbican: the semicircular Lion Tower, where the Royal Menagerie was housed from Henry III's time to 1834 (making the Tower England's oldest zoo). You then have to imagine a second drawbridge connecting the Lion Tower with the Middle Tower, the only surviving defences of the barbican. From the Middle Tower a causeway bridge leads over the Moat to the Byward Tower, the main entrance through Edward I's outer curtain wall into the Outer Ward. This entrance was closed by a portcullis, which can still be seen above. Beyond the Byward Tower is the Bell Tower, the south-western corner of Henry III's inner curtain wall.

The modern-day Tower Wharf, with its splendid park of antique artillery, makes it hard to realize that the Tower's second main entrance was by water, direct from the Thames. This was via the watergate: the famous 'Traitor's Gate' under St Thomas's Tower. Contrary to popular belief, Traitor's Gate is not of Tudor vintage (though most of the famous names who passed through it were). Like the rest of the outer curtain defences, St Thomas's Tower was built in the thirteenth century by Edward I.

The steps leading up from Traitor's Gate are directly in front of the main gatehouse tower piercing Henry III's curtain wall. This is the Bloody Tower (complete with portcullis), dominated to the right by the circular Wakefield Tower. The Bloody Tower's original name was the Garden Tower because it led to the Constable's garden in the Inner Ward; the 'Bloody' derives from the supposed murder there of the 'Princes in the Tower' (the young sons of Edward IV) on Richard III's orders in 1483. For good measure, the 8th Earl of Northumberland committed suicide in the Bloody Tower in 1585 – a grim blend of Tudor mythology and reality.

Through the Bloody Tower, the splendid mass of the White Tower dominates the Inner Ward in looming isolation – but it did not do so originally. A

The essence of Norman architecture : solid columns and rounded arches in St John's Chapel, White Tower.

look at the map is needed to understand the original layout. Extending eastward from the White Tower, a small bailey was anchored at its south-east corner on a bastion of the ancient city wall of Roman London. This has now disappeared. When Henry III enclosed the White Tower in his curtain wall, he also connected keep and curtain by running a wall north from the Wakefield Tower (parallel with the Roman city wall) and joined it to the White Tower with a twin-tower gatehouse (Coldharbour Tower). As the original entrance to the White Tower was on the south side and not, as today, on the north, it was therefore completely enclosed by an *Inmost Ward*. It only needed Edward I's outer curtain and barbican to complete an approach to the White Tower of appalling complexity (Lion Tower/Middle Tower/Byward Tower/Bloody Tower/Coldharbour Gate/White Tower): Plantagenet castle-building at its most ingenious.

Not even the beautifully displayed armour, weapons and other exhibits on view in the White Tower are more impressive than the enormous

The most famous Norman keep in England: London's White Tower, rising grimly beyond the river-front defences.

thickness of the keep's masonry. Look for the hallmark of the Norman tower keep: the massive cross-wall dividing the building in two. And on no account forget to visit the Chapel of St John in the White Tower, one glance at which will tell you more about the Normans and their architecture than a thousand books.

The Tower's attractions are well signposted and there is no need to describe them all here. Photography and sketching are permitted, 'provided no obstruction or nuisance is caused', but no photography is allowed in the Jewel House, a prohibition which can come as a bitter surprise to the unprepared. Appropriately enough, the best place from which to see the Changing of the Guard is the site of the Block, just north of Tower Green. Yeoman warders conduct regular guided tours, and the Tower also has good restaurant, snack bar and toilet facilities.

One final word of advice, particularly to visitors with young children. Close encounters with the famous Tower ravens are best avoided: an ingratiating croak has been known to be the prelude to a swift chop with a beak that can really hurt.

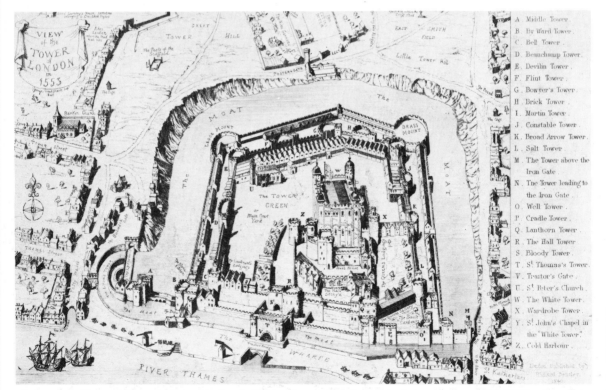

A plan of the Tower defences in 1553, showing the White Tower still joined to the inner curtain wall by Coldharbour Tower (Z) and the Wardrobe Tower (X).

SALTWOOD, KENT

Privately owned
1 mile (1·6 km) NE of Hythe;
A20/M20 from Maidstone/Ashford
or Dover/Folkestone

Saltwood is a privately-owned castle, so do not go along without checking opening times (normally Sundays and Bank Holidays from late May to September). Castle and grounds represent a joint triumph of Victorian castle preservation and subsequent private ownership; the grounds are very beautiful.

This castle is an Angevin reconstruction (1160) on an eleventh-century foundation and, like so many castles, is associated with one notorious event above all others. Though Saltwood technically belonged to the archbishopric of Canterbury, it became a front-line position in Henry II's fatal quarrel with Archbishop Thomas à Becket. Despite repeated requests from Becket, the King took no steps to prevent one of his more aggressive barons,

Rannulf de Broc, from establishing himself at Saltwood with a private army. They used Saltwood to store crops looted from the archbishopric's estates; but this crude persuasion failed to cow the defiant Archbishop. As the well-known power base of de Broc and his thugs, Saltwood was the rendezvous for the four knights who slipped away from Court, crossing the Channel to murder Becket and win the King's favour. It was from Saltwood that the conspirators rode to Canterbury on the day of Thomas à Becket's notorious martyrdom, 29 December 1170.

Subsequently confirmed as the property of Canterbury, Saltwood reverted to royal ownership 370 years later, when it was presented to Henry VIII by Archbishop Cranmer. By then the castle's value as a fortification had long since disappeared, though it had received several additions since the twelfth century. Of these the most important was the splendid fourteenth-century gatehouse – the residential part of the castle today. Saltwood is therefore a perfect example of how improved residential comfort often went hand-in-hand with improved defensibility.

Saltwood Castle in Kent as it looked before its reconstruction as a private residence, showing the imposing fourteenth-century gatehouse.

DEAL, KENT

Department of the Environment
By A258, 7 miles (11·3 km) NNE from Dover
or A257/A258 from Canterbury via Sandwich

Of the surviving 'stone battleships' built by Henry VIII, Deal is particularly impressive for two reasons: the shoreline it was built to command has remained stable over the centuries, and the castle itself was never converted to a residence to the extent of its neighbour Walmer. You therefore see this geometric masterpiece virtually as completed in 1540, under the spur of the French invasion scare of 1539. Deal was built at great speed (about 18 months) with masonry cannibalized from the dissolved Carmelite Priory, under the direction of Stefan von Haschenperg (Henry's 'Deviser of Buildings' from 1537 to 1543). Henry himself took an active part in designing his new fortifications, particularly their tapered gunports – 'splays as the king's grace hath devised'.

Deal was designed for all-round fire-power, with overlapping circuits of six semicircular bastions each commanding a 60-degree arc of fire. The castle was built to present as little and as low a target as possible, like a modern battle tank in a 'hull-down' position. It would have been impossible for enemy gunners to get a fair shot at the outermost walls, sunk below ground level in a deep dry moat, without coming under converging fire from the upper storeys. The moat floor is commanded by an unbroken ring of 53 gunports, again with overlapping arcs of fire; and a smaller ring of gunports commands the narrow ward or ditch separating the outer defences from the keep. Deal's defences are loopholed with over 145 ports for cannon and handguns. Few castles anywhere, of any period, have had so much fire-power built into them.

But notice how all the best medieval features are still present at Deal: fully concentric defences, with no entrance at moat-floor level apart from a postern to allow sorties; a single entrance at ground-floor level, with a main door impossible to attack without passing under five 'murder-holes'; and outer defences virtually impossible for attackers to convert, at any point, into a strongpoint for an assault on the inner defences. The only way to reach the keep

The approach to Deal, covered by embrasures and circular gunports in the outer gatehouse wall.

The floor of the moat was covered by interlocking lines of fire from the gunports.

Murder holes in the brick vault of the gatehouse.

entrance is by traversing one-third of an enclosed ward, every inch of which could be swept by fire, as could every inch of the wall of the keep. Underground store-rooms and the all-important well lie under the keep. And all designed for a garrison fewer than 50 strong.

Deal was garrisoned during the Armada crisis of 1588, and held for the King in the English Civil War. It surrendered, after two sieges, when all hope of relief had gone (August 1648), but was far too important to destroy, and remained an operational fortress for the rest of the seventeenth century. An interesting parallel with the Tower of London is that eighteenth-century attempts to extend Deal's living quarters were destroyed by German bombs in the Second World War, and omitted in subsequent restoration work.

DOVER, KENT

Department of the Environment

Dover marks the start of the transition from the Norman tower keeps of the eleventh and early twelfth centuries to the concentric castles of the thirteenth. Like the Tower of London, Dover is a 'growth' castle: a keep-and-curtain design with later improvements spanning four centuries, the last being added by Henry VIII.

There are no superlatives adequate for Dover: it has to be seen to be believed. When completed at the end of the twelfth century by Henry II's great architect Maurice the Engineer, Dover was one of the strongest castles in Christendom, and it still looks it. The might of the central defences is seen to excellent advantage because the keep and inner

Dover Castle complex, with Henry II's keep and inner curtain at the centre and the main entrance (Constable's Gate) at lower right.

curtain are not obscured by trees, as at the Tower of London. The castle is dominated by the enormous keep at its heart: basically a cube (98 ft by 98 ft/ 29·9 m by 29·9 m) set on a battered (inward-sloping) plinth, with square towers at each corner. The keep is ringed by Henry II's curtain wall, with ten rectangular flanking towers and two twin-tower gatehouses. Each of these gatehouses was originally

The main strongpoint of Dover's outer defences: the defiant sweep of Constable's Tower, enclosing the main gate of the same name.

The massive, cube-shaped block of Dover Castle keep, solidly based on a battered (inward-sloping) plinth.

protected by a barbican, of which only the northern one has survived.

An outer curtain, extended to the cliff edge, was added under King John in the thirteenth century. These new defences, with their D-shaped flanking towers, served Dover well during its most famous siege, by the French, in 1216–17, when the whole of south-east England from Lincoln to the Channel (including London and the Tower) passed temporarily under French control after the death of John. In this crisis, Hubert de Burgh's resolute defence of Dover, imperilling the French cross-Channel supply route and inspiring a growing resistance movement in the south, was vital in

persuading the French to cut their losses and quit England.

Unlike the Tower of London, whose outer curtain defences were completed under Edward I, Dover's defences reached their widest extent in the thirteenth century under Edward's father, Henry III. He abandoned John's northern gateway (which had been mined during the great siege) and built the splendid Constable's Gate on the west side – still the main entrance to Dover Castle today. The final modifications to Dover's outer defences – Henry VIII's bastions and the scarping of the east side for battery-fire defence – were made in the sixteenth and seventeenth centuries.

The Parliamentarians took Dover with comparative ease in the Civil War, but would have been most unlikely to have destroyed it even if it had resisted a bitter siege. Dover's magnificent state of preservation, as the cream of twelfth- and early thirteenth-century castle-building, was guaranteed down the centuries by the supreme importance of its site on the White Cliffs – 'the front door of England'.

ROCHESTER, KENT

Department of the Environment
A2 from London, Dartford; M2 from Dover,
Canterbury; A29/M2 from Maidstone

Ruined, floorless and roofless though it is today, Rochester is still a superb castle to visit. It is one of the most impressive Norman and Angevin tower keeps in all England, ranking with Dover and the White Tower at London. Rochester comes between these two in date: it was built in the latter years of Henry I, the Conqueror's youngest son, by William de Corbeil, Archbishop of Canterbury, who received the King's licence to build a 'fortification or tower' at Rochester in 1127.

Taller than either the White Tower or Dover, with a ground-to-parapet height of 113 feet (34·5 m) (the four flanking towers are 12 feet (3·7 m) higher), Archbishop William's tower keep was intended to transform the earlier castle at Rochester. Built between 1087 and 1089, this was the work of Bishop Gundulf, the Conqueror's Clerk of Works, whose greatest masterpiece was the White Tower. Like the White Tower, Gundulf's castle at Rochester used the old Roman city walls as foundations for the bailey defences, and these in turn were retained to screen Archbishop William's huge new tower keep.

Archbishop William's keep was no mere stronghold. It was intended to function as an archbishop's palace, with apartments and amenities for his retinue and guests. No other great castle of the period contains so many built-in facilities for a large civilian establishment (such as garderobes for sanitation, of which Rochester has an abnormally large number). On the second floor, the level of the Great Hall (notice the row of sockets for the massive floor-beams), the keep's defensive cross-wall was pierced with an arcade – making it useless for defence at this level, but adding greatly to the living space. You can still see the well-head running up the centre pier of this arcade, providing each floor of the castle with its own water supply. Thus Rochester is startling proof of how early the castle's basic role as stronghold was combined with its other role as lordly residence.

The castle chapel was not enclosed within the main walls, but instead was situated in the upper storey of a forebuilding extending from the north wall. The approach to the main door of the keep, below the chapel, was through an outer entrance

The tower keep of Rochester, showing the round flanking tower built to replace the one destroyed by mining in the 1215 siege.

tower at the side. This makes the forebuilding of Rochester keep a clumsy forerunner of the barbicans and tower gatehouses of later castles.

Yet Rochester's real problem was that too much trust was put in the strength of the keep without enough attention being given to the outer defences. Unlike, say, the Tower of London, Rochester was never taken in hand by a royal castle-builder tough enough to encroach ruthlessly on the surrounding township in order to give the keep an effective belt of concentric curtain walls. The rebuilding of Gundulf's curtain wall undertaken by Henry III, Edward III and Richard II was cosmetic rather than corrective. By 1400 Rochester was too obsolete to justify the expense of keeping it in repair, and was already far gone in decay. Though its mighty stone shell has survived five centuries, a glorious monument to Norman castle-building, the castle's rebuilt corner tower always bore witness to the vulnerability of tower keeps when inadequately screened.

WALMER, KENT

Department of the Environment
(For directions, see Deal, p. 30)

Walmer Castle is easy to find: 1 mile (1·6 km) south of Deal, to whose castle Walmer was the nearest link in Henry VIII's defence chain along the South Coast. The two make an interesting contrast because Walmer, unlike Deal, was extensively rebuilt in the eighteenth century to become the official residence of the Lord Warden of the Cinque Ports. The current incumbent is H M Queen Elizabeth the Queen Mother. The most famous of past Lord Wardens to live at Walmer was the Duke of Wellington, and the wealth of Wellington memorabilia at Walmer makes it an ideal visit for all fans of the Iron Duke who are also interested in castles.

Walmer is open daily, except for the brief periods when the Lord Warden happens to be in residence; and none of the reconstruction work which created its state rooms has erased or marred the basic layout of Henry VIII's castle, built at the same time as Deal (1539–40). Walmer has a much simpler layout than Deal, being a four-fold, instead of a six-fold, cloverleaf, with three tiers of guns to Deal's five. Walmer's round keep (also with well and storerooms at its core) is a simple masonry drum, without projecting bastions. But there is the same lowering of the castle's bottom tier below ground level, with gunports commanding the floor of a deep moat; and the same well-defended main gatehouse and death-trap courtyard between main wall and keep, designed to be swept by defensive fire.

The Wellington memorabilia (including the original Wellington boots) are on the first floor. In fine weather, visitors to Walmer can walk out of the Dining Room onto the gun platforms to enjoy the view from the northern and eastern bastions.

Modern gardens and Tudor gunports in the moat of Walmer Castle, today the residence of the Lord Warden of the Cinque Ports.

UPNOR, KENT

Department of the Environment
A228 from Chatham/Rochester via Frindsbury;
2 miles (3·2 km) from Rochester, signposted

Rochester and Upnor Castles lie so close together that both can be visited easily in a morning, and this is a most appropriate association. Rochester was one of the first stone castles built in England, and Upnor one of the last, some 450 years later, in the reign of Elizabeth I. Both had unhappy histories as defensive strongpoints, because each was the result of misapplied principles. Rochester was weak because it relied too much on the inherent strength of the tower keep, and lacked well-spaced outer defences. Upnor, on the other hand, owed its weakness to too much confidence in too little fire-power – the belief that the guns of a single small fort could render the tidal Medway impassable to a seaborne enemy. And both castles failed dismally, more than once, when put to the test.

Upnor's position still *looks* formidable enough, commanding the dog-leg in the Medway leading from the lower estuary to Chatham. The castle was really a blockhouse, built between 1559 and 1567 to secure the new Fleet base at Chatham, but it saw no action in Elizabeth's reign. In the Civil War it was held for Parliament from 1642 to 1648, when it was taken by men of Chatham dockyard in the King's name. This was less of a Royalist rising than a disgruntled riot, and it was a humiliating event for a strongpoint of such importance; the Royalist 'garrison' lost heart as soon as proper troops turned up and demanded their surrender.

As with Rochester's need for proper concentric defences after the great siege of 1216, Upnor's need after the Civil War was for the addition of flanking batteries to raise its fire-power. But what Upnor got was near-total neglect, paid for in abundance when the Dutch Fleet swept up the Medway (June 1667) to attack the English fleet there. Pepys' *Diary* tells how 'the good old castle built by Queen Elizabeth' did its feeble best, though the Dutch warships 'made no more of Upner's shooting than of a fly'; and that 'Upner played hard with their guns at first, but slowly afterward, either from the men being beat off [by Dutch landing parties] or their powder spent.' In true British style, the Medway stable-door was properly bolted *after* the fiasco of 1667, with the addition of downstream batteries making Upnor redundant.

Upnor Castle survived, with extensive modification, as a residence, but though it lacks the bristling menace of earlier Deal it is a most attractive Tudor castle, out of the ordinary and well worth a visit.

Built under Elizabeth I to protect the Fleet anchorage in the Medway, Upnor Castle proved to have too little fire-power to beat off the Dutch in 1667.

LEWES, EAST SUSSEX

Sussex Archaeological Society
A27 from Brighton; A259/A27 from Hastings
via Bexhill and Eastbourne;
A26 from Tunbridge Wells;
A275 from East Grinstead

Lewes is another first-generation Norman castle. It was the seat of one of William I's most trusted lieutenants, William de Warenne, who was granted extensive estates in Sussex after the Conquest. William de Warenne's castle was built to command the valley of the Sussex Ouse – as its contemporary, Roger de Montgomery's castle at Arundel, was built to command the valley of the Arun. How well Warenne succeeded may be judged from the superb views over the town and surrounding countryside which the visitor enjoys from Lewes Castle.

William de Warenne seems to have attempted a most ambitious novelty at Lewes: a castle centred on two mottes instead of the usual one. A more orthodox design was obviously chosen when the time came to convert the defences to stone, with a shell keep erected on only one of the mottes. Curtain defences were added in the thirteenth century, and an enormous barbican – the best-preserved part of the castle ruins today – in the early fourteenth.

The story of Lewes as an active castle ended unusually early, with the extinction of the Warenne line in 1347 and the depopulation of Sussex in the Black Death of 1348. In the years of recovery, Lewes Castle was eclipsed from the west by Arundel and from the east (after 1385) by Bodiam, remaining abandoned and increasingly ruinous, and used inevitably as a quarry by the townsmen. There was no halt to the process of dilapidation until the nineteenth century, when the Sussex Archaeological Society intervened to preserve what was left of this finely-sited castle.

Lewes Castle : a shell keep completed on only one of the original two mottes.

PEVENSEY, EAST SUSSEX

Department of the Environment
A259 from Eastbourne and from Hastings via Bexhill

Pevensey is a fine specimen of a 'hermit-crab' castle, with the walls of a Roman coastal fortress used as outer bailey defences for a Norman castle. Pevensey's Romano-British name was *Anderida*, and according to the *Anglo-Saxon Chronicle* it was stormed with great slaughter by the invading South Saxons in AD 491. That is the last recorded instance of Pevensey falling to a direct attack, for over the intervening 1,500-odd years, though often besieged and occasionally surrendered, Pevensey has never been taken by direct assault. This makes it a decided rarity among English castles.

After the Conquest, William I granted Pevensey to his half-brother, Robert de Mortain, who set about the conversion of the Roman defences into a castle. He began by building a simple tower keep in the south-eastern curve of the oval described by the Roman walls, enclosing this keep with a ditch and palisade to form an inner bailey. By 1088 Pevensey Castle was already strong enough to hold out against William II in the revolt against the new King by Count Robert's brother, Odo of Bayeux, until starved into surrender. King Stephen, besieging Pevensey in 1147, also failed to storm the castle because of the strength of its 'most ancient walls'. With the accession of Henry II in 1154, Pevensey became a Crown castle and the great years of

Pevensey's moat, and the north and east towers screening the inner bailey.

building began: a late twelfth-century keep with massive rounded projecting towers was added, and subsequently enclosed by a thirteenth-century curtain wall. This was studded with three D-shaped flanking towers and a twin-tower gatehouse.

Pevensey's two most famous sieges in its final form were against the supporters of Simon de Montfort in 1264 (holding out for Henry III) and against Richard II in 1399 (holding out for Henry, Duke of Lancaster, afterwards Henry IV). But despite its undoubted strength, records show that Pevensey was an expensive castle to maintain; this, combined with the receding of the sea coast which lessened the castle's strategic importance, led to a

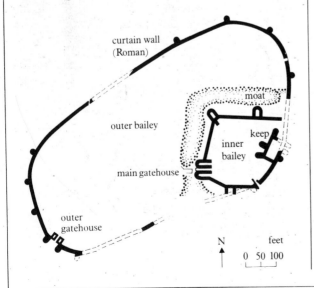

curtain wall
(Roman)

moat

outer bailey

keep

inner
bailey

main gatehouse

outer
gatehouse

N   feet
0 50 100

Pevensey Castle keep from the east, standing outside the circuit of the curtain wall of the Roman 'Saxon Shore' fortress.

story of sustained neglect from the end of the fourteenth century. By 1500 Pevensey Castle had been abandoned, and though surveyed in 1573 was dismissed as not worth the immense cost of repair. An emplacement for two guns was built behind the fallen wall of the outer bailey for the Armada invasion crisis of 1588, but there was no role for Pevensey in the English Civil War.

Pevensey's keep suffered worst from continual quarrying over the centuries, but the immense strength of the masonry has preserved most of the ancient Roman walls and the inner bailey curtain and towers. The castle's last private owner, the Duke of Devonshire, presented it to the nation in 1925, and preservation work began at last. In the Second World War, however, camouflaged machine-gun positions were sited among the ruins and a blockhouse (now removed) was built in the main entrance. Most of these twentieth-century defences were left deliberately, as witness to Pevensey's unique longevity as a stronghold.

The basement of Pevensey's north tower, in the inner bailey, with a separate stairway leading up the tower's interior.

BODIAM, EAST SUSSEX

National Trust
E of A229, 3 miles (4·8 km) s of Hawkhurst;
A21 from Tunbridge Wells, A229 from Maidstone,
A229 from Hastings, A267/A265 from Hailsham via Heathfield

*Inside the south-east drum tower at Bodiam. The square
holes supported the floor beams of the
upper storey.*

Bodiam has a unique place among English castles, and one look will tell you why. This is everyone's dream of a medieval castle – compact, symmetrical, with towers and battlements of a stone which looks particularly beautiful in late afternoon or evening sunshine, apparently floating at the centre of a wide encircling moat. Without the distractions of a bustling modern town on its doorstep, Bodiam seems timeless. If ever a castle makes readers of Malory think of Sir Lancelot's beloved castle, Joyeuse Garde, it is Bodiam.

Despite all appearances, Bodiam is more of a fortified manor than a castle. Its builder, Sir Edward Dalyngrigge, was licensed in October 1385 to 'fortify and crenellate his manor house ... and to construct and make thereof a castle in defence of the

adjacent countryside and for resistance against our enemies'. Like Henry VIII's coastal castles, Bodiam was built to block a French invasion which never came. The castle is a rarity; a strongpoint of national defence 'contracted out' by the Crown (or, in more depressing modern terms, defence on the cheap). Bodiam's new role also indicates the speed with which the ancient Cinque Port of Rye was, by the late fourteenth century, losing all value as a naval base for coastal defence. The new Bodiam Castle was intended to block any French advance inland from Rye up the Rother Valley.

Though never put to the test against French invaders, Bodiam's defences were shrewdly contrived. The wide moat kept the walls outside the effective range of the primitive cannon of the day;

*The spacious and elegant screen passage
flanking the lord's hall at Bodiam,
viewed from the north.*

Bodiam's wide moat would have prevented enemy siege gunners from bombarding the walls at point-blank range.

Bodiam was designed to be cannon-proof as well as mine-proof. The original causeway across the moat led first to a barbican (the remains of which can still be seen) then made a right-turn towards the castle gate. This last stretch of causeway was swept by the castle's own guns, firing through 'keyhole' ports built into the twin towers of the gatehouse. Yet Bodiam was always more of a residence than a fortress; the green courtyard of today was once packed with the lord's apartments, servants' quarters, store-rooms and kitchens, with most advanced chimney ducts built into the outer walls, and a generous allocation of windows.

Though hastily surrendered to the Parliamentarians in the Civil War, Bodiam was viciously slighted by the victors and remained a ruin for the next two and a half centuries. From 1917, Bodiam's fighting shell was painstakingly re-created at great expense under the direction of Lord Curzon, who presented this model of castle restoration to the nation in 1925.

The gatehouse of Bodiam Castle, flanked by 'keyhole' gunports for defensive fire, and with a restored portcullis above the gate.

ARUNDEL, WEST SUSSEX

Privately owned
A3100/A283/A284 from Guildford via Petworth and Pulborough;
A24/A29/A284 from Dorking via Pulborough; A27 from
Portsmouth via Chichester, from Brighton via Worthing

Arundel falls into the same category as the Tower of London and Windsor: a castle replete with attractions, for which too brief a visit is really a waste of time and money. It has been the residence of the Dukes of Norfolk for 500 years; when the 300-year-old Fitzalan dynasty became extinct in 1580, the castle and title passed to the Howard family.

The similarity between the layouts (and indeed the modern fabrics) of Arundel and Windsor is very striking. Both are extensive Victorian reconstructions of medieval linear castles, which were in turn extensions of first-generation motte-and-bailey castles with shell keeps. The restoration of Arundel was completed in 1903, and although the internal result is a particularly impressive masterpiece of the

The machicolated south tower at Arundel, part of the extensive rebuilding carried out under the Dukes of Norfolk in the nineteenth century.

The bridge across the ditch to the Bevis Tower at Arundel, showing how the curtain wall is angled sharply inwards to connect with the keep.

nineteenth-century Gothic Revival, the work started with the preservation of the twelfth-century shell keep on its motte and the thirteenth-century curtain wall and barbican.

Arundel, with a chalk spur commanding the valley of the river Arun, had been a natural site for a Norman motte-and-bailey. Its conversion to a stone castle began almost at once, and the most impressive survival from Arundel's first stone defences is the squat tower gatehouse, known as Earl Roger's Tower (named after Earl Roger de Montgomery, who died in 1094). The twin barbican towers screening Earl Roger's Tower were added, with the

Arundel Castle on its commanding ridge, viewed from the south-west across the river Arun.

outer curtain wall, by Richard, first of the Fitzalan Earls of Arundel (1289–1302). But this did not create a truly concentric castle, with the keep fully enclosed by the curtain wall. Arundel's western curtain wall is angled sharply inward to join the keep, leaving the latter as part of the outer defences – a notable weakness.

Arundel withstood two famous sieges in the twelfth century: one by Henry I attacking the rebel Earl Robert in 1102 (Arundel fell in three months), and one by King Stephen attacking his rival, Henry I's daughter Matilda (Arundel held out and Matilda escaped). But the castle's third and worst siege was in the Civil War. After its capture by the Royalists in December 1643 the Parliamentarians promptly besieged Arundel, before its new garrison had put itself in a proper state of defence. An unusually heavy series of artillery bombardments caused extensive damage to the western defences (you can still see the marks of Roundhead shot on the Barbican towers) and the Royalists surrendered on 5 January 1644. Arundel was then further wrecked by deliberate slighting and became steadily more ruinous until restoration work started with the 11th Duke in 1789. The painstaking work of restoring Arundel's medieval defences to their original appearance was the enduring achievement of Henry, 15th Duke of Norfolk, between 1890 and 1903.

Another fine result of the nineteenth-century rebuilding of Arundel: the Dining Room.

FARNHAM, SURREY

Department of the Environment
A31, 9 miles (14·5 km) W of Guildford;
M3 to Junction 4, then 7 miles (11·3 km) south
via Frimley, Farnborough, Aldershot, A3011

Farnham was one of the more important manors of the medieval bishopric of Winchester. The first Farnham Castle in stone was one of five built without Crown licence by Henry of Blois (Bishop of Winchester 1129–71) during the civil wars of his brother King Stephen. This square stone keep on a conical motte was destroyed by Henry II in 1155. There is no documentary evidence for the rebuilding of Farnham Castle as a shell keep ringed by a curtain wall, but this seems to have been accomplished, this time very much under royal licence, between about 1180 and 1200.

This is the oldest part of Farnham Castle as it stands today, and it is extraordinary on two counts. Firstly, most of the old masonry is quarried local chalk – the least suitable of all materials, one might think, from which to build a castle. This chalk is

Though clad in a seventeenth-century façade with nineteenth-century additions above, the core of Farnham Castle gatehouse is of medieval origin.

either rubble bound with mortar (as in the foundations of the original keep) or blocks faced in later years with sandstone or brick, which explains the 'patchy' look of Farnham's masonry. And the second surprise is the shell keep itself – enclosing the whole motte instead of merely crowning it, with the gap between shell wall and motte later filled in. By about 1300 the gap had vanished, filled to the level of the top of the motte, creating a massive drum-like structure. The keep's central well-shaft (which can still be inspected) was sunk through the heart of the now-buried motte. The outer face of the keep is studded with six shallow, rectangular flanking towers reminiscent of Framlingham, with the south-eastern tower doubling as the keep's gatehouse.

The wedge-shaped area of the original bailey was preserved in the outer walled courtyard, around which were packed the living apartments, hall, kitchen and chapel appropriate to a bishop's household. Entry to this complex is via the splendid brick tower built by Bishop Waynflete in 1470–5,

The entrance to the keep at Farnham Castle is a murderous bottleneck equipped for portcullis defences and overhead fire through a murder hole.

The keep of Farnham Castle, an original motte enclosed in a shell wall, with the interior subsequently filled in.

probably inspired by the contemporary brick masterpiece of Tattershall.

Farnham surrendered to the invading French in the war of 1216–17, but was recaptured ten months later (March 1217). In the Civil War, Farnham was taken and briefly held by the Royalists (November 1642), then recaptured and held by the Parliamentarians until January 1645, when Royalist raiders surprised the garrison and took possession for a day before retreating. Being held by Parliament for most of the war did not, however, save Farnham's keep from being slighted (deliberately wrecked) in 1648 'so as not to be defensible or tenable by an enemy if surprised'. (The resultant gap can be seen on the east side.) Farnham returned to the bishopric of Winchester with the Restoration of 1660. It remained the residence of the bishops of Winchester until 1927, and of the bishops of Guildford until 1955 – a continuous occupation which happily saved this fine castle from further decay.

OTHER CASTLES TO VISIT

Allington, Kent
Finely restored late thirteenth-century reconstruction on earlier site; today owned by Carmelite Order.

Chilham, Kent
Polygonal twelfth-century keep; gardens only open to public.

Eynsford, Kent
Impressive twelfth-century curtain wall; only $\frac{1}{2}$ mile (800 metres) N of Lullingstone Roman Villa.

Hever, Kent
Finely restored fourteenth-century fortified manor, of Henry VIII/Anne Boleyn fame.

Sissinghurst, Kent
Tudor fortified manor, more mansion than fortifications. Beautiful gardens.

Guildford, Surrey
Shell of Norman keep.

Bramber, West Sussex
Much-slighted twelfth-century castle of former great prominence on south coast – a noted 'leaning tower' castle.

Hastings, East Sussex
Cliff-top shell of stone replacement for William I's first castle on English soil.

THE SOUTH COUNTRY

DONNINGTON, BERKSHIRE

Department of the Environment
1½ miles (2·4 km) NW of Newbury;
B4494 from Newbury, A34 from M3, Junction 13

Donnington is a castle of the same vintage as Bodiam: a fortified manor of the late fourteenth century, brought into being by licence of Richard II in 1386. It was the scene of one of the longest and most dramatic sieges of the Civil War, during which the main part of the castle was battered to destruction. Only the twin-tower gatehouse has survived, but it dominates the landscape for miles.

Donnington was a manor in Saxon times, as attested by Domesday Book. In 1386 it was held by Richard de Abberbury, a knight in the service of Edward the 'Black Prince' who had been chosen as one of the young Richard II's guardians, subsequently serving at the royal Court as chamberlain to Queen Anne. This service earned him Richard's licence to 'build anew and fortify with stone and lime, and crenellate a certain Castle on his own land at Donyngton'. The result was an oblong curtain wall enclosing the manor buildings and courtyard, with round flanking towers at the corners and a square flanking tower halfway along each of the long sides. These outer defences were completed after the magnificent, three-storey tower gatehouse, of

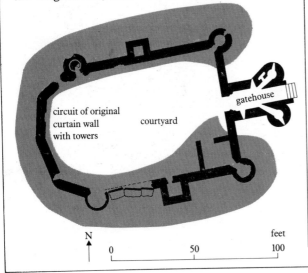

circuit of original
curtain wall
with towers

courtyard

gatehouse

N

feet

0   50   100

which two cylindrical towers have survived virtually intact. The remnants of outer barbican walls can be seen outside the gatehouse entrance.

Unscathed by the Wars of the Roses, in 1568 Donnington earned a visit from Queen Elizabeth I, for which the old drawbridge before the barbican was replaced by a fixed bridge. In 1586 Camden's *Britannia* described Donnington as 'a small but very neat castle, seated on the banks of a woody hill, having a fair prospect and windows in all sides very lightsome'. But this attractive picture was shattered for good by the Civil War. In September 1643 King Charles sent Colonel John Boys to garrison Donnington (abandoned by its Parliamentarian owner) with 200 foot, 25 horse and guns. Boys's first task was to employ local labour to surround Donnington with earthworks and artillery bastions in the latest style. In this he succeeded so well that Donnington resisted five successive Parliamentarian sieges and bombardments between July 1644 and March 1646. The castle was twice relieved by the King's army and Boys, knighted by a grateful monarch, launched repeated sorties against the Parliamentarians.

By the spring of 1646, however, Donnington's garrison was in poor shape. The whole of the curtain wall and its towers had been battered to rubble, leaving only the gatehouse standing. There was no hope of further relief; but Boys did not surrender until he had passed an envoy through the Parliamentarian lines to obtain the King's written permission to do so. Only then did Boys make his surrender, receiving the full honours of war, on 1 April 1646. Donnington's garrison marched out 'bagge and baggage, muskets charged and primed, mache in Coke, bullet in mouthe, drumes beatinge and Collurers ffleyinge. Every man taken wth hime as much amunishion as hee could Carrye. As honourable Conditions as Could be given.'

The twin towers of Donnington's gatehouse – all that was left from the Civil War siege which battered the rest of the castle to ruins.

WINDSOR, BERKSHIRE

M4 from London, Reading to Junction 6; A308 from Staines;
A332 from Camberley; A355 from Beaconsfield via Slough

Windsor has two overriding claims to fame: it is the biggest inhabited castle in the world, and the only royal castle to have been used continually as such for the past 500 years. England's only other royal castle of similar size and antiquity, the Tower of London, is the finest concentric castle in England; Windsor is England's finest linear castle, with the baileys or wards enclosed in a row instead of one inside the other.

Windsor started life in the aftermath of the Norman Conquest as one of the cordon of castles sited by William I to cover the approaches to London and the south-east, his original power base in England. The site on the ridge above the major waterway of the Thames was an important one, and the lie of the land permitted two baileys, one higher than the other. This layout is preserved today in Windsor's Upper and Lower Wards, with the keep on its motte – the Round Tower – enclosed by the Middle Ward.

Though Windsor's intimate connection with the royal family has made it probably the best-known and most popular English castle today, it would have been a very different story eight centuries ago. Easily the most hated element of Norman supremacy was the strict preservation of all forests as royal hunting estates, with savage punishment meted out to any who dared hunt the king's game or fell the trees which sheltered it. Hunting remained the true 'sport of kings' throughout the Middle Ages (even the saintly Edward the Confessor was a fanatical huntsman) and Windsor became a favourite hunting lodge of the Norman kings.

Henry II began both the improved fortification of Windsor (shell keep and curtain wall) and its conversion into a royal residence. By 1193 Windsor, seized by the rebel Prince John during his brother Richard's imprisonment in Germany, was strong enough to sit out a siege by forces loyal to Richard. Windsor was King John's headquarters during the tense negotiations leading to the signing of Magna Carta at nearby Runnymede in June 1215, and was again successfully defended in a three-months' siege during the civil war which followed. These were Windsor's only two sieges, and the damage inflicted by them was speedily repaired by the strengthening of the defences and expansion of the royal apartments under Henry III in the thirteenth century.

By 1300 Windsor had reached a stage of development that would be familiar to modern visitors, and the castle was a favourite royal residence. But its great days as a national institution began in the fourteenth century with the reign of Edward III, the first of the only two English monarchs born at Windsor (the other being Henry VI). Edward III fostered what might be called the national cult of St George, embodied in his foundation of the knightly Order of the Garter which has had its seat at Windsor ever since. The Order's glorious Chapel of

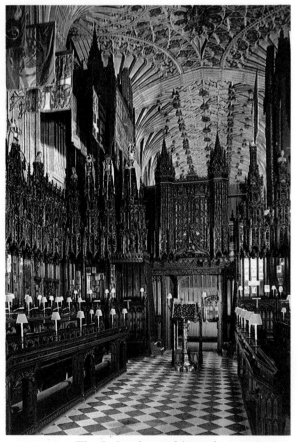

*The glorious fan vaulting and
heraldic banners of
St George's Chapel.*

The superb skyline panorama of Windsor Castle, dominated by the Round Tower, with St George's Chapel to the left.

St George, one of the most beautiful buildings in England, was begun by the Yorkist King Edward IV in the late fifteenth century and completed by Henry VIII in 1528. Henry VIII also ordered the building of the imposing main entrance familiar to visitors today.

Windsor was lucky in the Civil War: it could easily have gone the way of Donnington, destroyed in repeated sieges, but instead was held for Parliament throughout the war and never attacked. Charles I was confined there in December 1648 before being transferred to London for his trial and execution in the following month. So far from consigning Windsor to oblivion, the regicides unwittingly helped enhance Windsor's royal aura by burying the 'Martyr King' there. The restored Charles II held summer court at Windsor, where the royal apartments were again rebuilt and redecorated; later Windsor was the favourite residence of George III (1760–1820), who was buried there, setting a precedent followed by every English monarch since.

Windsor's magnificent appearance today is due primarily to the much-maligned George IV (1820–30). Determined to rebuild the castle as a sumptuous and imposing modern palace, he gave the architect Jeffry Wyatville that most difficult of tasks, to transform without destroying, and took a close personal interest in the work. Wyatville's triumphant success ranks as one of the greatest achievements of English nineteenth-century architecture. He rightly concentrated on the Round Tower as the heart of the castle, and managed to double its height without making the result grotesque. You have to look very hard to see the join between Henry II's shell keep and Wyatville's addition, the latter with its circuit of machicolation (projecting arches) unobtrusively suggestive of a royal crown. Another master-stroke was the choice of facing stone for the outer walls, which looks natural and timeless, rather than sham.

Like the Tower of London, Windsor merits more than a short visit. The State Apartments in the Upper Ward are not always open to the public, and it is worth checking in advance because they should not be missed. Military buffs must not overlook the Queen's Guard and Waterloo Chambers; Queen Mary's Dolls' House always delights young children; and it should be unthinkable to visit Windsor without at least entering St George's Chapel.

The Long or Queen's View at Windsor, looking from

the Great Park towards the State Apartments.

PORTCHESTER, HAMPSHIRE

Department of the Environment
6 miles (9·6 km) from Portsmouth,
off A27 to Fareham/Southampton

Portchester is the most complete 'hermit-crab' castle of the late eleventh and early twelfth century. It lies on the north shore of Portsmouth Harbour, whose waters still protect the east wall at high tide. The castle's outer bailey walls are those of the best-preserved of all the late Roman 'Saxon Shore' fortresses built along the east and south coasts in the third and fourth centuries AD. The medieval castle dates from Henry I's reign (1100–35) and seems to have been built under his supervision. The north-eastern corner of the Roman walls was replaced with an exceptionally fine twelfth-century tower keep, enclosed by a rectangular inner bailey. The inner bailey walls were protected by a right-angled moat crossed by a drawbridge.

In its heyday, Portchester's capacious Roman walls accommodated a small town. Eventually the town grew too big for the confining walls and began to migrate to the more spacious site of present-day Portsmouth; but for 300-odd years Portchester remained one of the most important royal castles of the Norman and Angevin kings. Its unique position, with 'one foot on shore and one on sea', made it ideal for mustering and embarking armies destined for service in Normandy. Edward III shipped his army from Portchester for the Crécy campaign of 1346, and Henry V did the same for the Agincourt campaign of 1415. In many ways, Portchester was a miniature duplicate of the Tower of London; the keep was used as both state treasury and state

Portchester Castle, with a twelfth-century keep and inner bailey built into an angle of the Roman 'Saxon Shore' fortress.

The enduring masonry and drum-shaped flanking towers of the outer, late Roman walls at Portchester.

prison, and Richard II built a palace within the inner bailey.

Yet Portchester's role as an effective royal castle was cut short with surprising speed; as early as 1441 it was written off as 'ruinous and feeble'. There were two real reasons for Portchester's redundancy: its continuing eclipse by nearby Portsmouth, and the more fundamental problem that there was no way of up-dating the defences to bring it into line with more modern developments in fortification. It remained virtually a ghost castle until Charles I sold it off to private ownership in 1632. Held for Parliament throughout the Civil War, Portchester suffered the ignominy of being used as a barracks. But the castle was still leased back by the Crown for use as a prisoner-of-war camp in the Dutch Wars of the later seventeenth century, the Seven Years War in the eighteenth century, and the Revolutionary and Napoleonic Wars.

A fascinating castle to visit, if only because of the great antiquity of its defences, Portchester shows Norman ingenuity in castle-building at its best. It is a unique specimen of a twelfth-century castle which, with results fatal to itself, failed to evolve.

The unusually complete tower of Portchester's twelfth-century keep.

HURST, HAMPSHIRE

Department of the Environment
A337/B3058 to Milford on Sea from
Southampton via Lyndhurst;
approach to castle by ferry from Keyhaven,
or on foot from Milford on Sea, 2½ miles (4 km)

Hurst Castle is one of Henry VIII's 'intermediary' coastal castles, built between the French invasion scare of 1539–40 and the French descent on the Isle of Wight in 1545. Of all Henry VIII's castles it is the one with the most spectacular site, if less directly accessible by car than most of the others. American visitors will probably think of Fort Sumter at Charleston. Although Hurst does not stand on a natural island, like Sumter, it has an equally commanding position: out at the end of a 2½-mile (4-km) shingle spit extending into the western entrance to the Solent from Milford on Sea, at the Solent's narrowest point.

With Calshot, 12 miles (19·3 km) north-east at the entrance to Southampton Water, Hurst Castle represents the first stage of Henry VIII's plan to render Southampton and Portsmouth secure from assault by sea. It is unlikely that the King ever believed that this could be done merely with forts like Hurst, sited only on the mainland. But it needed the stimulus of the French invasion of 1545 – in which Hurst played no part – for the building of additional defences on the Isle of Wight. Hurst's later counterpart across the Solent on the Isle of Wight, creating an unpleasant crossfire against any enemy fleet attempting to penetrate the Solent from the west, was Yarmouth. The complementary role intended for Hurst and Yarmouth may be compared with that of Pendennis and St Mawes in Cornwall.

Hurst was held for Parliament in the Civil War and at the end of 1648 served briefly as a prison for Charles I during his transfer from Carisbrooke to Windsor, London and execution. Always a fighting castle pure and simple, Hurst lacked any apartments fit for royal visitors and Charles was deeply depressed by his dank and gloomy surroundings. Pondering on the chances of assassination during his stay at Hurst, Charles bitterly called the castle 'a place fit for such a purpose'.

Subsequent modifications to the castle are the result of Hurst's enduring service as a coastal strongpoint over four centuries. Its excellent site caused it to be manned again in both world wars.

Henry VIII's castle at Hurst, thrust out into the narrows of the western Solent at the end of a narrow spit of shingle.

OLD SARUM, WILTSHIRE

Department of the Environment
A345, 2 miles (3·2 km) N of Salisbury

Old Sarum is like Portchester: a 'hermit-crab' Norman castle planted amid fortifications of an earlier age, which lost its strategic value when the town it was intended to dominate migrated to a new site. It is a useful reminder that medieval castles never existed in isolation, but were woven tightly into the social fabric of the age. Any dramatic changes at local level inevitably resulted in change to the local castle – in the case of Old Sarum, a terminal one.

Old Sarum is first and foremost a Celtic fortification, but it does not seem to have been a Roman township. Sarum's old ramparts were certainly defended again in AD 552, when the West Saxons defeated a Romano-British force there – a reminder of how long it took Roman Britain to give way to the invading Anglo-Saxons. As a Saxon township or *burh*, fortified to survive in the long wars against the Danes, *Serebrig* was important enough for kings to hold court there, and to be assigned a mint. But Old Sarum Castle followed the Norman Conquest.

Military genius that he was, William I never overlooked a geographically useful site, and his attention seems to have been drawn there before 1070, when he disbanded his army at Old Sarum after crushing the Northern Rebellion. In 1075 he chose it as the new seat for the old bishopric of Sherborne, which stretched from Windsor to Lyme Regis. The new cathedral was begun at Old Sarum and completed in 1092 – promptly to be destroyed in a storm. In the reign of Henry I, Bishop Roger of Sherborne, one of the great administrators of the Norman era, planned a permanent replacement not only for the cathedral but also for the motte-and-bailey castle which had occupied the centre of Old Sarum since the 1060s.

Like the bull's-eye of a target, Bishop Roger's new castle dominated the circular enclosure within the old Celtic ringwork, with a deep circular dry ditch surrounding a broad motte crowned with a circular curtain wall. Unlike Pevensey or Portchester there was no keep at Old Sarum, but the stout outer wall of the Bishop's Palace, taking up the north-western quadrant of the inner bailey, was clearly intended to serve the same purpose as the walls of the Pevensey and Portchester keeps. What made Old Sarum startlingly different from other castles of the same date was the fact that the Bishop's Palace was completed *first*, with the curtain wall being completed later in the twelfth century. There are very strong parallels between Old Sarum and Bishop Roger's other castle, Sherborne, also built between 1107 and 1139.

Old Sarum was neither a fortified cathedral town, nor a fighting castle equipped with apartments and suited to a leading civilian role, but a wholly experimental mix of the two – and the experiment did not work. At Old Sarum, Church interests prevailed over the military. The cathedral clergy bitterly objected to living almost like prisoners, under the jurisdiction of the castle. In 1219 not only royal but papal approval was given for the building of a new cathedral – the birth certificate of modern Salisbury. The rapid development of the new cathedral town left Old Sarum Castle high and dry, stripped of the dual role which Bishop Roger had built into it a hundred years before. By the mid-thirteenth century, with its existence now futile and its maintenance costs soaring, Old Sarum was already withering on the vine – just as Portchester was to do, for almost precisely the same reasons, 200 years later.

When visiting Old Sarum, it is fascinating to speculate as to what would have happened to the castle's development without its fatal connection with the cathedral. For here, inside the ancient Celtic ringwork, may be seen the first, fumbling attempt at a concentric castle layout – a failed experiment a century ahead of its time.

Like the bull's-eye of a target : Old Sarum keep, protected by ditch and low motte, surrounded by the ancient Celtic ringwork enclosing the cathedral site.

CARISBROOKE, ISLE OF WIGHT

Department of the Environment
1 mile (1·6 km) sw of Newport;
buses from Newport to Yarmouth and Freshwater;
local bus service to castle in summer months

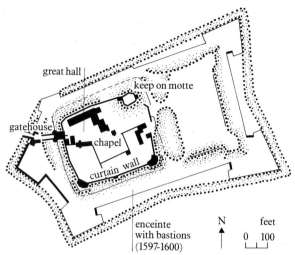

The imposing gatehouse of Carisbrooke Castle, thrusting outward from the western curtain wall.

Doubtless Carisbrooke Castle will always be associated with the ten-month captivity of Charles I in 1647–8, after the final defeat of his cause in the English Civil War. But it is also a perfect model of the evolution of English castle history, from its beginnings in the eleventh century to the seventeenth.

As the Isle of Wight's most important castle, Carisbrooke has the unusual distinction of having been kept in excellent repair for nine centuries without a break. The castle began as a standard Norman motte-and-bailey, constructed by William FitzOsbern in the 1060s. Between 1107 and 1136 this was converted to a stone shell keep and curtain wall, in the form of an oblong with rounded corners spliced to the motte and keep at the north-western corner. These defences were unusually strong because of the height of the steep banks sloping away outside the curtain wall; there was no need for a ditch or moat. A chapel, great hall and other service accommodation were added in the thirteenth century, when the north-east curtain wall was strengthened, and a barbican was added to the gatehouse through the western wall. This was converted to a typically fourteenth-century twin-tower gatehouse in 1335–6.

Carisbrooke's defences were overhauled so as to fit the castle for the 'cannon era' in the last 13 years of the sixteenth century, the work beginning at the time of the Armada crisis (1587–8). The south-east and south-west towers of the curtain wall received pointed outer bastions, and a completely new set of enclosing ramparts was built round the entire castle, with 'arrow-head' artillery bastions at the corners. These final embellishments completed Carisbrooke Castle as it appears today.

Carisbrooke's medieval history was uneventful; it only stood one siege, by King Stephen's forces in 1136, in which it sustained little damage because its water supply failed, forcing the rebel Baldwin de Redvers to surrender. In the fourteenth century the Hundred Years War gave rise to a succession of

The Governor's House at Carisbrooke (now the Isle of Wight Museum) with the castle keep on its motte in the left background.

Looking down from Carisbrooke's keep and motte to where the eastern curtain wall resumes its circuit.

attacks by French raiders, all of which were beaten off. At the outset of the Civil War the Royalist Governor, the Earl of Portland, was neatly removed by order of Parliament before he could garrison Carisbrooke for Charles I, and the Parliamentarians retained the castle throughout the war.

The irony of Charles I's famous imprisonment at Carisbrooke is that he went there voluntarily, after escaping from Hampton Court in November 1647. The Governor was the nephew of one of the King's chaplains and Charles believed him to be a Royalist sympathizer at heart. But any sympathy the Governor might have had was dispelled when he discovered that Charles was secretly negotiating to renew the Civil War with the aid of an invading Scottish army. From then on (December 1647–September 1648) Charles remained a prisoner at Carisbrooke, making a hopeless bungle of an enterprising plan to free him (which failed when Charles discovered, too late, that the bars on his bedchamber window were too narrow for him to squeeze through!).

One of the most famous sights of Carisbrooke is the donkey-powered windlass drawing water from the well in the courtyard. This was added during the castle's final expansion in the reign of Elizabeth I.

YARMOUTH, ISLE OF WIGHT

Department of the Environment
A3054 from Newport; B3401 from Carisbrooke

Yarmouth was one of Henry VIII's last castles, built to supplement the Isle of Wight's defences after the French invasion of 1545. It was sited so that with Hurst, on the other side of the Solent, it could subject any enemy attempt to penetrate the western Solent to a punishing crossfire.

Yarmouth presents a total contrast to the rounded 'cloverleafs' of Deal and Walmer. It marks the mid-sixteenth century transition from rounded bastions to the straight-sided fortifications of the late sixteenth and seventeenth centuries, which reached their peak of development with the French military engineer Vauban in the reign of Louis XIV. The new vogue for straight-sided fortifications exploited the fact that cannons fire in straight lines, and that a correctly angled fortress layout relying on straight lines required fewer guns to defend it than one with rounded bastions. This, of course, was a refinement of a principle which had dominated castle design from its medieval beginnings: the fact that a symmetrical castle layout required a smaller garrison than an unbalanced one. Yarmouth's original garrison was a master gunner, a porter, and 17 soldiers.

The layout of Yarmouth is simplicity itself: a canted square, with the north-western corner pointing out to sea and the south-eastern, inland corner protected by an 'arrow-head' bastion. Two triangular gun platforms were added to the seaward corner in about 1632 to increase crossfire against attacks from the sea.

Like Carisbrooke, Yarmouth had a Royalist commander at the outbreak of the Civil War but surrendered on demand, and remained in Parliamentarian hands throughout the conflict. The castle remained a coastal battery throughout the late seventeenth and eighteenth centuries, and the Napoleonic Wars. It was finally disarmed in 1885, used as a Coast Guard signalling station until 1901, and commandeered for service use in both world wars, extending its active life to 400 years.

The courtyard of Henry VIII's castle at Yarmouth, looking west to the stairway leading up to the main gun platform.

CHRISTCHURCH, DORSET

Department of the Environment
A35 from Bournemouth, Southampton;
A337 from Lymington;
A338/B3347 from Salisbury via Ringwood

Christchurch was originally a first-generation motte-and-bailey, sited, like Arundel and Lewes, to command the lower reaches of a river – in this case the Avon – on the Channel coast. Although it is extensively ruined and there is comparatively little to see, Christchurch is still worth a brief visit when passing through the Bournemouth region. For this is a rare example of a square stone keep – not a shell keep – built on an earlier artificial motte, and the twelfth-century walls have survived. The other important surviving unit is the Castle Hall, or Constable's House, which was built in the castle bailey (now the gardens of the King's Arms Hotel) at the same time as the keep, instead of being a later addition. Though roofless, the enormously thick walls of the Constable's House show that it was built as a 'mini-keep': part of the defences of the castle, not merely living quarters. The hall itself, with original windows and round chimney, is on the first floor. Here, then, is an unusually early example of improved defensibility and domestic comfort advancing together.

*A window in the shell of
the Constable's House, in the bailey of
Christchurch Castle.*

There is a strong parallel between Christchurch and Old Sarum, and it is to be found in the town's famous Norman priory close by the castle. This is another example (as at Old Sarum and, above all, at Durham) of an important piece of Church property taking precedence over the local castle, and effectively preventing it from evolving further than its twelfth-century stage of development.

Christchurch Castle keep from the south-east – a most unusual example of a stone keep built on an earlier, artificial motte.

CORFE, DORSET

Privately owned
A351 from Wareham

Corfe is the Old English word for 'gap' or 'pass', in this case describing the natural gap in the range of hills traversing the peninsula known as the Isle of Purbeck, south of Wareham. The castle stands on a natural hillock commanding the gap, and was the site of a royal residence long before the Norman Conquest. At Corfe, on 18 March 978, the young King Edward 'The Martyr' was murdered – allegedly at the instigation of his stepmother Elfrida, in order to put his half-brother Ethelred 'The Unready' on the throne. The *Anglo-Saxon Chronicle* lamented that 'no worse deed than this for the English people was committed since first they came to Britain'. At Corfe the murder is still commemorated by the massive, twin-towered gateway known as the Martyr's Gate, built on the reputed scene of the crime.

The Martyr's Gate was probably the outer entrance to the keep built at Corfe by William 1; but the castle evolved rapidly on this natural site, with a lower ward being added outside the upper. What you see today are the ruins of the castle's near-total rebuilding in the late fourteenth and early fifteenth century, the Martyr's Gate now being the gatehouse between the Lower and Upper Wards. The result was an immensely strong linear castle, which shares with Pevensey the rare distinction of never having been taken by assault.

In the twelfth century, long before it had reached its full strength, Corfe had joined the list of castles unsuccessfully besieged by King Stephen in the wars of the Anarchy. Corfe later added to its notoriety by becoming the favourite castle of King John. Here, John is said to have starved to death 22 French nobles who had backed the claim to the throne of John's nephew Arthur. It was also at Corfe

Corfe seen from the east, showing the long wall enclosing the castle's lower ward.

The shattered but still magnificent King's Tower at Corfe, victim of particularly thorough Parliamentarian slighting after the Civil War.

that John strung up a local prophet, Peter the Hermit, who had been so unwise as to forecast the King's downfall; before his execution the unfortunate Peter was dragged to Wareham and back on a hurdle.

Remaining in permanent occupation, Corfe survived the Wars of the Roses and in 1572 was granted to Sir Christopher Hatton, one of Queen Elizabeth's favourite young men. Hatton not only repaired the defences to meet the Armada crisis but considerably expanded Corfe's amenities as a Tudor mansion. But the castle's finest hour was its magnificent defence by Lady Bankes in the Civil War, from August 1644 to February 1646. When the siege began, Corfe was the only remaining Royalist stronghold between London and Exeter; but the castle remained a thorn in the side of the Parliamentarian cause for another 18 months. When Corfe fell – to treachery, after a fifth column had been slipped inside the walls during negotiations – Parliament wasted no time in exacting an efficient revenge, voting for the castle's demolition within the week (5 March 1646).

The resulting work, carried out more ruthlessly than with any other Parliamentarian slighting, destroyed the keep (King's Tower) to such an extent that its original layout can only be guessed at. Yet even when the wreckers had done their worst, Corfe could not be deprived of the rugged splendour which still awaits the visitor today.

The solid-looking gatehouse of Sherborne Old Castle.

SHERBORNE, DORSET

Department of the Environment
A30 from Shaftesbury, Yeovil; A352 from Dorchester;
A357/A3030 from Blandford Forum

Sherborne has two castles, but only one is a medieval site. The new castle dates from the sixteenth century and was built by Sir Walter Raleigh when he found it impossible to convert the old castle to a mansion. (There is a story that Raleigh was enjoying a quiet smoke in the garden of the new castle when a servant, terrified by the novelty of tobacco, hurled water over his master in the belief that he was on fire.)

Sherborne Old Castle was built by Bishop Roger in 1107–39, and the keep defences are very similar to those of its contemporary, Old Sarum: more of an enclosed courtyard, a prototype inner ward, than the usual square or rectilinear keeps of the period. It is easy to see why the twelfth-century chronicler William of Malmesbury, praising Bishop Roger's genius as an architect, wrote that his buildings seemed to be carved from a single stone.

Though Old Sarum Castle suffered the most from the transfer of the bishopric from Sherborne in 1075, the evolution of the latter castle was also cramped by the flourishing Abbey which remained on the site of the former cathedral. In the Civil War Sherborne suffered a similar fate to Donnington, undergoing two destructive sieges and taking a heavy battering from the Parliamentarian artillery. It finally surrendered on 15 August 1645, and was at least spared further extensive slighting.

OTHER CASTLES TO VISIT

Southsea (Portsmouth), Hampshire
Coast-defence castle of Henry VIII, from which he watched *Mary Rose* go down in 1545.

Old Wardour, Wiltshire
Late fourteenth-century fortified manor, twice besieged in Civil War; fine gardens.

Portland, Dorset
Coast-defence castle of Henry VIII.

The courtyard of Sherborne Old Castle, showing the extensive remains of the early twelfth-century stronghold.

THE SOUTH-WEST

NUNNEY, SOMERSET

Department of the Environment
A361, 3 miles (4·8 km) sw of Frome

Nunney is one of the most impressive fortified manors in the whole of England. Like Bodiam, built slightly later, the castle today is reduced to its curtain-wall shell. This features four enormous round towers at the corners, each crowned with a ring of machicolations (projecting arches through which missiles could be dropped on attackers at the foot of the wall). But Nunney has few of the graceful, balanced proportions of Bodiam; in plan it seems to have been squeezed together like a concertina to fit on a small, raft-like island skirted by a moat only 30 feet (9·1 m) wide. Reduced to its essentials, Nunney consists of two pairs of flanking towers connected by walls 40 feet (12·2 m) long. It has a look suggestive of many French châteaux of the fourteenth century, and was in fact built in 1373 by Sir John de la Mare with the proceeds of loot from the French wars.

A comparison of Nunney with Bodiam shows how rapidly warfare was changing in the late fourteenth century, for Nunney is clearly a 'pre-

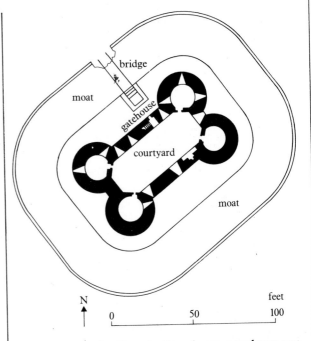

cannon' castle. Bodiam, built only 15 years later, not only has a wide lake-moat to force enemy gunners to shoot at extreme range, but it is also equipped with gun-ports through which to shoot back. Lacking both these amenities, Nunney was left in poor stead when defended by the Royalists during the English Civil War. With no defence in depth as at Donnington or Corfe, Nunney surrendered after a mere two-day bombardment. The Nunney garrison could certainly have held out much longer by retreating up the towers, which would have endured a good deal of battering; but there was no heart in the defence. The last Royalist field army had been broken at Naseby three months before, there was no possibility of relief, and the commander offered an easy surrender if he could be retained in command afterwards. The offer was rejected, but happily the early surrender spared Nunney from slighting on anything like the scale of Corfe.

The military threat of Nunney's tower machicolations is belied by the large windows in the connecting curtain walls.

The modest moat offered little real security to the walls of Nunney.

FARLEIGH HUNGERFORD, SOMERSET

Department of the Environment
A366, 3 miles (4·8 km) w of Trowbridge

Farleigh Hungerford is a straightforward fortified manor house of the late fourteenth century, square in outline with two wards. The principal surviving buildings are the tower and the extremely interesting chapel, with its weapons, armour, effigy tombs and fifteenth-century wall paintings. The castle was built between 1370 and 1380 by Sir Thomas Hungerford, steward to John of Gaunt, Duke of Lancaster, and second Speaker of the House of Commons.

The most scandalous story attached to Farleigh Hungerford relates to the tower, in which an early Tudor Hungerford kept his third wife locked up for four years on suspicion of infidelity. He tried to kill her by poison and starvation, neither of which succeeded, and was himself executed by Henry VIII for treason *and* unnatural vice, in that order.

The Hungerfords, a family noted for political acumen, managed to keep their property out of the crossfire during both the Wars of the Roses and the English Civil War. But the castle fell into ruin together with the family, and in 1689 was gambled

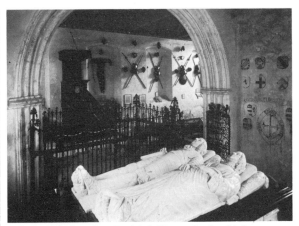

The family chapel at Farleigh Hungerford, with its weapon displays, tomb effigies and wall paintings, is not to be missed.

away with no fewer than 27 other manors by Edward Hungerford, who died in poverty. Subsequently it was neglected until its preservation in the nineteenth century, when picturesque ruins became part of fashionable taste.

The fourteenth-century fortified manor of Farleigh Hungerford, looking across the courtyard towards the gatehouse and chapel.

BERRY POMEROY, DEVON

Privately owned
1½ miles (2·4 km) s of A381, Newton Abbot/Totnes,
or 1 mile (1·6 km) N of A385, Totnes/Paignton

The ruins of Berry Pomeroy Castle, cloaked in woodland on the edge of a ravine, should not be visited on a bright sunny day. They are seen to best advantage in dark and ominous weather. For Berry Pomeroy is one of the most mysterious castles in the country: no one knows for sure how it came to its end, and the ruins are haunted.

Berry Pomeroy takes its name from the de la Pomerai family which held it until 1548, when the castle was sold to Edward Seymour, Lord Protector in the minority of Edward VI. Under Elizabeth I and the early Stuarts, the Seymours spent prodigious sums in converting Berry Pomeroy's apartments into what was, by all contemporary accounts, one of the most splendid and luxuriously furnished private mansions in the country. The castle escaped damage or destruction in the western campaigns of the Civil War, and seems to have reached a zenith of splen-dour in the reign of James II (1685–8). In November 1688 William of Orange, after landing at Brixham with his army, stayed at Berry Pomeroy at the start of his march to London and the Crown. But at some unspecified date over the next 12 years Berry Pomeroy was completely destroyed in a disastrous fire. There was fearful talk of the castle having been set ablaze by lightning, which in that witchcraft-haunted century carried immense overtones of divine or diabolical wrath. Commenting on the mystery in his *Worthies of Devon* (1701) the vicar John Prince wrote merely that 'all this Glory lieth in the Dust, buried in its own Ruines'.

Four of Berry Pomeroy's ghosts deserve special mention. There is Henry de Pomerai, one of the castle's founding fathers, who committed the most unknightly deed of killing a herald and later stabbed himself to death. Margaret de Pomeroy was locked up and starved to death by a jealous sister for falling in love with the same man. Another woman was killed with her lover by an outraged brother when caught at a secret tryst. But most to be feared is another lady ghost who walks in the woods. She killed her illegitimate baby, and appalling luck befalls all who see her.

The gatehouse of ghost-ridden Berry Pomeroy Castle, mysteriously destroyed by fire in the seventeenth century.

DARTMOUTH, DEVON

Department of the Environment
A380/A381/B3207 from Exeter via Newton Abbot
and Totnes; A3022 from Torbay with ferry

Few English south coast ports have a longer naval tradition than Dartmouth, where fleets mustered for the Crusades of the twelfth century, the French wars of the fourteenth, and the D-Day armada in 1944. There are two castles at Dartmouth, one of which is a ruined coastal blockhouse built in 1481. The more interesting of the two, however, is about 100 years older. It was built in Richard II's reign (1377–99) to defend the Dart estuary against raids from the sea. Strictly speaking, this older Dartmouth Castle is not a true castle, in that it was never a royal or lordly residence, or designed for a permanent garrison; but it is included here as one of the best examples of how medieval fortifications were, from the late fourteenth century, adapted to the advent of cannon.

Like Tintagel in Cornwall (p. 75) Dartmouth Castle shows that medieval castle-builders did not invariably look for the likeliest high ground, then build on top of it. This is a strongpoint tailored to the face of the cliff, with landward security provided by the cliff itself. The fortifications consist of a 'V' of battlements 110 feet (33·5 m) across at the base, pointing out towards the estuary, with a squat tower at the squared-off point. The tower was built to mount guns firing through large rectangular openings, rather than the 'keyhole' ports which were modifications of the traditional arrow-slit.

At Dartmouth, therefore, we find England's oldest coastal battery, in startling contrast to the traditional appearance of the contemporary Bodiam. Despite their manifest differences Dartmouth and Bodiam are both examples of Richard II's flair for securing 'defence on the cheap', Bodiam being built as a licensed fortified manor, and Dartmouth by the town corporation.

Though it must be repeated that Dartmouth was not a true castle, it had all the hallmarks of the most effective English castles – above all adaptability for a long service life. Its value in coastal defence saved it from peacetime neglect, or deliberate slighting in the Civil War; the curtain wall was pierced with eight embrasures for additional fire-power in the eighteenth century, and it served in both world wars.

Dartmouth Castle, tailored into the cliff face on the west bank (left in the picture) of the river Dart to command the seaborne approach to the port.

TOTNES, DEVON

Department of the Environment
A38/B3210 from Plymouth;
A380/A381 from Exeter via Newton Abbot;
A381 from Salcombe, Kingsbridge

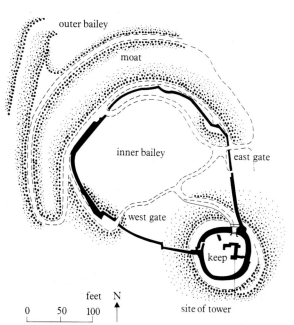

Totnes town stands at the head of the navigable reaches of the river Dart, at the junction of three valleys, and was therefore a natural site for a castle after the Norman Conquest. The first lord of Totnes, Judhael, was a Breton high in the favour of William I, by whom he was granted over a hundred manors in Devon. To command the town, Judhael built up a natural knoll into a castle motte, rendering it waterproof by sheathing it with clay and adding a pear-shaped bailey below. In its surviving form, Totnes Castle preserves the complete outline of Judhael's defence perimeter, right down to the stone foundation of the original wooden donjon on top of the motte. The ditch which formerly ringed the foot of the motte is now filled in and incorporated into the small gardens of the houses which cluster round the entire south side of the motte. As usual, visitors must imagine the castle uncluttered by the tall old trees obscuring the view over the bailey on the north side and the town houses built right up to the foot of the motte on the south.

Though never attacked or besieged, and devoid of military value long before the Civil War, Totnes Castle was an unusually active pawn in West Country medieval power politics. It passed through no fewer than eight changes of ruling family between the late eleventh century and the early sixteenth. The castle's conversion to a stone shell keep and walled bailey began under Reginald de Braose in 1219, but the work was poorly executed and soon became ruinous. The much more solid stonework visible today is the result of a complete rebuilding by William de la Zouch, on the orders of Edward II in the last year of his reign (1326–7). This reconstruction effectively preserved Totnes as one of England's most perfect shell keeps with a complete set of crenellations, the larger ones pierced for archery. From the keep's intact walkway visitors enjoy superb all-round views over Totnes town and the south Devon countryside.

A classic fossil specimen of the Norman motte-and-bailey: the shell keep at Totnes, with merlons pierced for defensive fire.

OKEHAMPTON, DEVON

Department of the Environment
A30, between Launceston and Exeter

Okehampton Castle stands on a knoll about half a mile west of the town, on the lower slopes of northern Dartmoor, and its extensively ruined state is the result of over three centuries of use as a local quarry. Though long overgrown, its fine site is now kept clear and rendered well worth a visit when travelling to or from Cornwall along the Exeter–Launceston road.

The castle began as a twelfth-century motte-and-bailey, converted to stone in the thirteenth century. Lying as it did far from the sea or the turbulent frontier zones of the Welsh and Northern marches, Okehampton was always more of a residence than a fighting stronghold. It was the original seat of the powerful Courtenay family and its ruins reveal a high proportion of residential buildings. The castle's further development was cut short when the Courtenays moved their family seat to Powderham Castle at Kenton in the 1390s.

Already badly run down, Okehampton Castle was finally abandoned after the execution of Henry Courtenay, Marquis of Exeter, by Henry VIII on a trumped-up treason charge in December 1538. The dominant element of the ruins today is, as usual, the keep. The configuration of the site suggests that if the Courtenays had stayed at Okehampton this castle could well have developed on the lines of Corfe, with upper and lower wards extending down the hill, though it would never have achieved the same massive strength.

The splintered ruins of the keep of Okehampton Castle, family seat of the powerful Courtenays until their move to Powderham in the late fourteenth century.

RESTORMEL, CORNWALL

Department of the Environment
1½ miles (2·4 km) N of Lostwithiel, A390 from
St Austell and Liskeard; B3269 from Bodmin

Though none of its outer defences have survived, Restormel is nevertheless one of the most beautifully proportioned shell keeps in England. The first castle was built by Baldwin FitzTurstin in about 1100 to command the crossing over the river Fowey; the conversion to stone defences began under Robert de Cardinan at the end of the twelfth century, with extensive inner development about 50 years later under Richard of Cornwall, contemporary with the rebuilding of Launceston.

The main strength of Restormel was clearly not the height of the motte, but the enormous width (50 feet/15·2 m) and depth of the ditch. The keep itself is one of the biggest of its type in the land, being some 50 feet wider in diameter (outer wall to outer wall) than those at Totnes and Launceston. This yielded space for generous accommodation within the keep: the walls of these inner chambers are still standing, giving Restormel the distinctive plan view of a spoked wheel. The chambers are ranged round the circular inner courtyard on two levels, the ground level being reserved for guardroom and storage. The entire upper storey was reserved for the lord of the castle and his family, with the chambers of the lord and lady on the north-west sector being faced by the hall on the south-east. The square tower jutting out to the north-east was the castle chapel. The sockets for the floor-beams of the upper storey can still be seen, as can others on the outer wall, below the parapet. These were to support *hoards* – temporary wooden galleries rigged in time of siege, from which attackers could be bombarded at the foot of the wall.

Other curiosities at Restormel include the deep underground chambers in the outer courtyard, the lord's private stair from the chamber south of the chapel to the walkway, and, in the hall beyond, the vertical speaking-tube built into the wall, leading up to the walkway. The kitchen beside the hall served food via a hatch in the wall and had a generous built-in fireplace – a remarkably advanced facility for a castle of this period.

Restormel had been abandoned long before the Civil War but, unlike most West Country medieval castles, briefly held a Parliamentarian garrison. This was speedily ejected by the Royalist army of Sir Richard Grenville in 1644, but the castle saw no further action. The skill with which the castle site, long overgrown, was cleared, has preserved one of the most interesting of all English castles of the thirteenth century.

The elegant shell keep of Restormel : looking towards the castle entrance on its low, broad motte.

PENDENNIS, CORNWALL

Department of the Environment
Falmouth – A39 from Truro,
A393 from Redruth, A394 from Helston

Pendennis Castle is another of Henry VIII's gun platforms, begun in 1539 and magnificently sited on Pendennis Point, the peninsula extending south-east of Falmouth town. Together with St Mawes across the water to the east, Pendennis was built to defend Falmouth and the fine anchorage of Carrick Roads.

It is a concentric circular castle, without the 'cloverleafs' which distinguish Deal and Walmer. The lie of the land, with a steep drop to the sea which the castle's guns were intended to sweep, ruled out 'sinking' the castle in a deep moat, but the upper gun embrasures were rounded to deflect shot. The keep was given splayed ports for 13 guns firing on two floors; and at ground level the curtain wall was pierced with 14 embrasures. An outer block-house, known as 'Little Dennis', was built at the very tip of the promontory.

Pendennis was transformed in the last five years of Elizabeth's reign, after a damaging Spanish raid

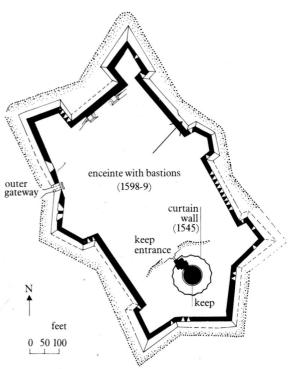

*The Tudor Royal Arms, fulsomely displayed
at Pendennis over the gateway
to the keep.*

on Penzance had given timely warning that Pendennis would hardly be able to repel a similar attack in force. Henry VIII's castle was girdled with an *enceinte*, or connecting rampart-with-bastions for extra artillery, with a steep-sided ditch all round; Little Dennis was similarly strengthened. In this new guise, as the most modern and best-armed castle held by the Royalists, Pendennis earned the undying fame of being the last English castle to surrender in the Civil War of 1642–6.

Untouched by the earlier campaigns in the staunchly Royalist West, Pendennis played host to Queen Henrietta Maria and Charles, Prince of Wales, before receiving the full weight of the Parliamentarian onslaught under General Fairfax in March 1646. The ensuing five-month siege re-iterated the lesson that any beleaguered castle or strongpoint is only as strong as the will of its garrison commander. Colonel John Arundell, Governor at Pendennis, was 70 years old and had seen

Henry VIII's keep at Pendennis. The approach bridge and original castle entrance are on the landward side, to the left.

Queen Elizabeth review her troops at Tilbury in Armada year (1588). Undeterred by the precipitate surrender of neighbouring St Mawes on 12 March 1646, Arundell told Fairfax that 'I will here bury myself before I deliver up this castle to such as fight against His Majesty'. After Arundell rejected a second surrender demand on 17 April, Fairfax ordered the close blockade of Pendennis by land and sea. Hunger, not enemy force, beat Pendennis in the end, though Arundell held on until the last hope of receiving relief and supplies had gone. He finally surrendered on 17 August 1646, his emaciated garrison marching out with the full honours of war.

Pendennis was much too important a coastal stronghold to be slighted after the Civil War. It remained in service, housing VIP state prisoners and enemy prisoners-of-war, and was manned in both world wars.

The southernmost extremity of the Pendennis defensive perimeter: the blockhouse of Little Dennis, perched above the water at the headland's tip.

ST MAWES, CORNWALL

Department of the Environment
A390/B3287/A3078 from St Austell;
A39/B3289 from Redruth

This is the smaller partner of Pendennis, built by Henry VIII in 1540 to create a crossfire against enemy ships trying to break into Carrick Roads. The castles face one another, and each can plainly be seen through the gunports of the other.

In March 1646 St Mawes surrendered to the Roundheads without firing a shot, leaving the Pendennis garrison to win glory in a famous siege; but this comparison is not really fair. St Mawes was always the poor relation of Pendennis. St Mawes was a much smaller castle, and when the time came to strengthen the defences of Pendennis in the 1590s, the cost of keeping 400 workmen employed on the new outworks for 18 months could not be duplicated across the water at St Mawes. As a result St Mawes remained more of a blockhouse than a castle fit for all-round defence, and was wholly unequipped to fight off an attack from the landward side, especially by the veteran army of Fairfax.

A gunner's eye view of St Mawes through a Pendennis gunport, showing how the two castles were intended to keep Carrick Roads closed to enemy shipping.

St Mawes Castle is not only smaller than its partner Pendennis, but was never given the outer defences necessary to endure a full-dress siege.

Scandalous though it will always remain to fanatical Royalists, the prompt surrender of St Mawes preserved what is probably the most attractive of Henry VIII's smaller castles. It is a mirror-image of the round keep of Pendennis, complete with rounded-edge embrasures to deflect shot. St Mawes remained in service as a coastal blockhouse for the next 300 years, and was manned again for service in the two world wars.

TINTAGEL, CORNWALL

Department of the Environment
A395/A39/B3266/B3263 from Launceston via Camelford
and Trewarmett; A39/B3263 from Bude via Boscastle;
A389/B3266/B3263 from Bodmin via Camelford and Trewarmett

As the locals would cheerfully agree, Tintagel is the centre of the 'King Arthur industry' and has been for the past 800 years, ever since Geoffrey of Monmouth wrote his *History of the Kings of Britain* (1136). This splendid romance tells how Arthur was conceived at Tintagel by the lovely Duchess Ygerna of Cornwall, after the arts of Merlin the enchanter had smuggled King Uther Pendragon through the castle's impregnable defences, disguised as the Duke. In the late fifteenth century Sir Thomas Malory, hauling all the Arthurian and Holy Grail legends together in his immortal book *Le Morte d'Arthur*, described the saviour of Britain as having been born at Tintagel as well as conceived there. More recently, the splendidly convincing 'Merlin' trilogy of Mary Stewart has brilliantly refurbished the Tintagel connection with Arthur. The legend lives on, as does the debate as to whether or not a 'real' King Arthur ever existed.

The hard facts are few, but well enough established. A perfectly credible sequence of Anglo-Saxon victories over the demoralized British, all in Kent, Sussex and Hampshire, is recorded in the *Anglo-Saxon Chronicle* from AD 445 to 530, when the West Saxons took the Isle of Wight. Then there is a most interesting 20-year gap before the next Saxon victories in the south and west. This gap coincides with the early Celtic stories of Arthur's great victory (at 'Mount Badon', wherever that may be) which stopped the Saxons in their tracks and won the British peace for a generation. If the British war leader who cut through the Anglo-Saxon record of conquest *was* called Arthur, there is no reason at all why he should not have been born at Tintagel (or, for that matter, buried at Glastonbury, where the monks supposedly discovered his tomb in the Abbey precincts in about 1190). But it is absolutely certain that the surviving castle ruins at Tintagel date from the twelfth and thirteenth centuries and can have no direct connection with a British war leader of the early sixth.

Tintagel Castle was built in about 1145 by Reginald, Earl of Cornwall, bastard son of Henry I. It is England's earliest linear castle built in stone,

The modern bridge over the vanished causeway, providing access to the curtain wall and inner ward of Tintagel Castle.

Though the legends endure, the surviving ruins of Tintagel's thirteenth-century defences have no possible connection with any real King Arthur.

The gateway and curtain wall securing Tintagel's inner ward. Holes in the wall once supported fighting platforms for the garrison.

with lower, upper and inner wards in a row; but its exploitation of the spectacular local landscape makes it like no other castle in the kingdom. This landscape consists of a steep headland, connected by a knife-blade of rock to a small island. The castle is divided between the mainland and the island, with the restricted landward approach and sheer cliffs all round making it impossible either to mine or to take by storm.

Like the shell keeps of Launceston and Restormel, Tintagel passed to Earl Richard of Cornwall in the early thirteenth century and he extensively rebuilt the castle; today's ruins date mainly from this reconstruction. The access paths used by modern visitors were built after 1852, when Tintagel was opened to a public fired with Arthurian fantasies by Tennyson's blank-verse *Morte d'Arthur*. The original narrow causeway connecting the upper ward with the inner ward on the island no longer exists, but the modern pathway still gives a vivid idea of what an enemy would have had to face, fighting his way across, no more than two or three abreast, under an arrow-storm from the inner ward's embrasured curtain wall. No wonder Geoffrey of Monmouth, who clearly knew the place, decided that Uther Pendragon must have used magic to get in.

Immensely strong though it undoubtedly was, Tintagel was also exposed to the eroding force of the Atlantic gales and must have been a prohibitively expensive castle to maintain. Tintagel's trouble was that it was too remote a castle to be worth the money.

By the mid-fourteenth century it was already ruinous and, after a last bout of invasion-scare repairs in Richard II's reign, the castle was finally abandoned in the fifteenth. From then until the Victorians set about preserving the remains, Tintagel was left wide open to dilapidation by local quarriers – who took full advantage of it – and relentless battering by the gales of 400 north Cornish winters. One of the biggest surprises about Tintagel is that there is so much still to see at this rugged and most beautiful castle site on one of the wildest parts of England's shoreline.

Tintagel : the upper and lower wards are on the mainland to the left, with a knife-blade of rock leading to the inner ward on the 'island'.

LAUNCESTON, CORNWALL

Department of the Environment
A30 from Exeter/Okehampton, Bodmin;
A388 from Plymouth, Holsworthy;
A384 from Tavistock

Launceston has always been one of the major gateways between England and Cornwall, and when William I assigned Cornwall to his half-brother Robert of Mortain in the post-Conquest settlement, Robert made Launceston his administrative centre. The town occupies a natural ridge, on which Robert's engineers threw up an immense earth motte at the north-east corner of a square bailey.

A fine aerial view of Launceston Castle. The round keep is enclosed by a shell on top of the original Norman motte.

Only three sections of the original bailey perimeter have survived intact – the enclosed area of the bailey is represented by the present-day Castle Green – but the shell keep on Earl Robert's motte still shows visitors what an unusually strong motte-and-bailey site this was.

As at Totnes, the shell keep was built in two stages, the first being a simple circular wall in the twelfth century. The main defences which the visitor sees today were the work of Henry III's younger brother Richard (Earl of Cornwall 1227–72). Earl Richard was one of the richest and most powerful men in thirteenth-century England – the country's only serious candidate for election as Holy Roman Emperor. On his orders, that great rarity, an English *cylindrical keep*, was built inside the existing shell keep. The result was a total novelty, one of the most imaginative and unusual strongholds to be found anywhere in England. Launceston's transformed keep not only embodied the increasing contemporary interest in concentric defences (which was actually making the traditional role of the keep redundant), but it also anticipated the multi-level fire-power built into Henry VIII's castles by some 300 years.

The new round tower contained two chambers one above the other, connected by a spiral staircase leading to a fighting parapet above. The gap between the tower and the shell wall was roofed over, providing a second firing platform for archers and crossbowmen. Outside the shell wall, a now-vanished outer wall screened yet a third firing platform at the foot of the keep defences, whose circular cross-section enabled the garrison to concentrate its fire-power with ease at the main point of any attack. Nor were the bailey defences neglected. Two of its new gatehouses have survived. The one at the foot of the motte staircase was originally fitted with two portcullises, while the keep itself was defended by a third portcullis at the top of the staircase. The other gatehouse, through the southern bailey wall opposite the car-park, has traces of outer barbican defences.

Though overhauled on the orders of Edward the Black Prince, who became the first Duke of Cornwall in 1337, Launceston had become badly run down by the reign of Elizabeth. A description in 1584 records that 'This triple crowned mounte, though abandoned, retayneth the forme, but not the fortune and favour of former times'. But more than enough 'forme' was left for Launceston to be garrisoned for Charles I in the Civil War, during which the castle eventually changed hands four times. Extensive damage was caused in the process, but this at least saved Launceston from further deliberate slighting after the war.

Launceston remained the seat of the local assizes

The keep at Launceston, showing how the shell wall round the later round tower provided the defenders with three levels on which to fight.

until 1840, when they were transferred to Bodmin. The noisome town jail in the bailey was then thankfully removed and the present gardens laid out. Quakers will not need reminding that their founding father, George Fox, was jailed at Launceston in 1656 for distributing 'seditious' tracts (also for refusing to take off his hat when hauled before the court).

OTHER CASTLES TO VISIT

Dunster, Somerset
Fortified manor, extensively rebuilt from sixteenth to nineteenth centuries; owned by Luttrell family since 1375.

Taunton, Somerset
Extensively rebuilt stronghold of the town's defence by Parliament in the Civil War. Houses excellent County Museum.

Compton, Devon
Fourteenth-century fortified manor, extensively rebuilt in nineteenth century; owned by Gilbert family since 1329.

Lydford, Devon
Castle begun in 1195 to dominate spectacular Lydford Gorge; mainly thirteenth-century remains.

St Michael's Mount, Cornwall
Spectacular island (at high tide) castle, originally a Benedictine priory; besieged in both Wars of the Roses and English Civil War.

EAST ANGLIA

CASTLE HEDINGHAM, ESSEX

Privately owned
1 mile (1·6 km) N of Sible Hedingham;
A604 from Colchester via Halstead;
B1058 from Sudbury; A1017/A131 from Braintree

Castle Hedingham is a privately owned castle, open to the public on Bank Holidays and three afternoons a week from May to September. It is a magnificent twelfth-century tower keep of three storeys, standing almost 100 feet (30·5 m) high and dominated by two corner turrets, built in about 1140 to command the crossing over the river Colne, 17 miles (27·3 km) upstream from Colchester. The bridge over the ditch, across which the castle is reached, is a much later addition of about 1500.

Castle Hedingham dominated one of the many estates held in East Anglia by the earls of Oxford, the de Vere family, which had a turbulent medieval history. Richard de Vere fought for Simon de Montfort at the Battle of Lewes (14 May 1265), in the civil war against Henry III. In the Wars of the

The massive twelfth-century arch spanning the Great Hall at Castle Hedingham. The restored flooring gives a vivid idea of life in these looming strongholds.

The fine tower keep of Castle Hedingham, dominated by its two corner turrets. The first storey main gate is approached by a stairway on the left.

Roses the family fought for Lancaster, with a notable lack of success. In February 1462 John de Vere, the twelfth earl, and his eldest son were sentenced for treason by the Yorkist Earl of Worcester, Constable of England, and executed. Eight years later, in the Lancastrian backlash which temporarily restored Henry VI, John, the thirteenth earl, had the satisfaction of passing the death sentence on Worcester in turn. But this was the same de Vere who helped lose the Battle of Barnet for Lancaster in April 1471, by losing his bearings in a fog and attacking the troops of his own side!

While at Castle Hedingham, do not miss the Church of St Nicholas – another masterpiece of Norman architecture of the twelfth century, built about 50 years after the castle.

COLCHESTER, ESSEX

Borough of Colchester
A12 from London via Chelmsford and Ipswich;
A134 from Sudbury; A604 from Harwich

Colchester prides itself on being 'Britain's oldest recorded town', and with good reason: it has seen a remarkable continuity of occupation since the Bronze Age. The Romans called it *Camulodunum* and built an enormous temple here to the Emperor Claudius, whose legions had launched the Roman invasion of Britain in AD 43. Alfred the Great's son Edward, advancing north-east from the Thames to drive the Danes out of East Anglia in the early tenth century, built a rampart round Colchester as a fortified town or *burh*. It was to be expected that the Normans would not overlook Colchester's value as the southern anchor of East Anglia. At Colchester they built the only stone tower keep other than London's White Tower to date from the reign of the Conqueror. And not the least of Colchester's claims to historical fame is that it boasts the most enormous castle keep not only in England, but in Europe.

Colchester was built by Eudo, *dapifer* or steward both to William I and to his two sons, William II and Henry I. As with the White Tower at London, Eudo's castle was sited in the old Roman city. In a way Colchester ranks as a 'hermit-crab' castle because, while not making use of standing Roman walls for its outer defences, the Norman castle nevertheless occupies a Roman site: the massive plinth foundation of the long-destroyed Temple of Claudius, which can still be seen beneath the castle vaults.

Colchester's Great Keep measures a staggering 171 feet by 146 feet (52·1 m by 44·5 m), yielding a ground area 63 per cent bigger than that of the later keep at Dover; and although only two of the castle's original four storeys have survived, it is still an impressive fortress. The castle was involved in a few dramatic actions in the Middle Ages, being surrendered during the French occupation of the south-east in 1216–17 and again during the Peasant's Revolt of 1381. Its finest hour came in 1648, during the renewed fighting of the Second Civil War. Stubbornly defended by the Royalists, Colchester beat off the attacks of Fairfax and the veterans of the New Model Army from 13 June to 28 August, when Sir Charles Lucas was forced to capitulate. The Parliamentarian general, incensed

Colchester Castle, the biggest twelfth-century great keep in Europe, built on the site of the Roman temple of Claudius.

The doorway at Colchester.

by what he regarded as a wanton shedding of blood, showed none of the chivalry he had displayed at Pendennis in 1646: the surrender terms were harsh and Lucas and another Royalist commander were shot. But not even Roundhead vengeance could level Colchester's great keep. Today it houses the fascinating collection of the Colchester and Essex Museum.

HADLEIGH, ESSEX

Department of the Environment
A13 from Basildon and Southend-on-Sea;
castle is 1 mile (1·6 km) w of BR Leigh-on-Sea

Hadleigh Castle lies in a small enclave of open country, hemmed in by the urban sprawl of Canvey Island and South Benfleet to the south and west, and Leigh and Southend to the north and east. Though extensively ruined, the castle still preserves the main layout of an early thirteenth-century manorial castle – the transition period from keep-and-curtain to fully concentric designs. It was begun in 1231 on one of the south Essex estates of the great Angevin crown official Hubert de Burgh, Dover's defender against the French in the war of 1216–17, and justiciar of England during the early reign of Henry

III. Though he never lost the popular aura of a national hero, Hubert was still a greedy and ambitious man, who at the peak of his power held estates in 15 counties. But he fell from royal favour in 1232, his estates were confiscated, and Hadleigh Castle was finally completed later in Henry III's reign.

Despite its apparently useful site overlooking the northern shore of the Thames estuary, Hadleigh never flourished as a castle worthy of sustained expense in maintenance. It is notable for having served as a temporary home for Anne of Cleves after she was divorced by Henry VIII. Nearly 200 years later, having been reduced to thoroughly picturesque ruins by ground subsidence, the castle became a favourite subject for the landscape painter John Constable. One of Constable's most powerful studies of Hadleigh Castle is in the Tate Gallery in London.

The castle as landscape ornament in the Romantic period : one of John Constable's studies of Hadleigh Castle's ruins commanding the Essex flatlands.

ORFORD, SUFFOLK

Department of the Environment
A12/B1084 from Ipswich via Woodbridge;
A12/B1078 from Saxmundham via Wickham Market

Lying only 12 miles (19·3 km) from Framlingham, Orford Castle (completed about 30 years earlier) is another Suffolk masterpiece of a twelfth-century castle – but in near-total contrast. These two are a perfect demonstration of how completely different neighbouring English castles of the same period could be. This difference is epitomized by the only parts of the two castles to have survived. At Framlingham the curtain wall and flanking towers have outlived the domestic buildings inside. At Orford the original outer curtain and towers have vanished, leaving only the splendid tower keep, the combined defensive and residential core of the castle. Again, Framlingham was a baronial castle, the fortification of which was actively restrained by Henry II. The King wanted no nearby rival to his splendid new creation, the royal castle at Orford.

Orford is unique because it is the earliest English castle for which detailed documentary evidence of the construction has survived. This evidence is preserved in the Pipe Rolls, the cash-flow records of the royal exchequer. They show that between 1165 and 1173, when it was completed, Henry II spent more money on Orford than on any other castle. Henry built Orford fast, with no expense spared, because on his accession there had been no royal castles in East Anglia, and he wanted to keep the powerful Hugh Bigod in check. Orford Castle immediately proved its worth by holding out in 1173–4 during the rebellion of Henry's eldest son, Henry 'The Young King'. Bigod not only backed the Young King but brought over an army of mercenaries from Flanders – who kept well away from Orford, however. Though briefly surrendered to Prince Louis of France in the war of 1216–17, Orford remained a royal castle until 1336, when Edward III granted it in perpetuity to Robert de Ufford, Earl of Suffolk. As with Framlingham, East Anglia's adherence to the Parliamentarian cause saved Orford from battle damage in the Civil War.

Orford Castle represents attempts to strengthen keeps by rounding off the corners which, without the alternative development of concentric castles, would have resulted in many more cylindrical

A masterpiece from the reign of Henry II: Orford's polygonal keep, the core of one of the strongest royal castles in East Anglia.

keeps. But though Orford's keep stands in splendid isolation today, it is important to remember that the bailey curtain wall and towers that screened it originally completed a defensive complex scarcely less formidable than Henry II's later achievement at Dover. These bailey defences were still more or less intact in 1600, but decayed steadily over the next 200 years. (The last section of the bailey wall collapsed 'with a tremendous crash' on the night of 1 July 1841.)

The weirdest story connected with Orford is that of the 'Orford Merman', dredged up in the nets of local fishermen in the 1170s and hauled to the castle for examination. He is described in a contemporary chronicle as 'naked and like a man in all his members', covered with hair and with a long shaggy beard. 'Whether he would or could not, he would not talk, although oft-times hung up by his feet and harshly tortured.' Given this brutal taste of life ashore, it is hardly surprising that 'later on, being negligently guarded, he secretly fled to the sea and was never afterwards seen.'

FRAMLINGHAM, SUFFOLK

Department of the Environment
A12/B116 from Ipswich via Wickham Market;
A45/A1120/B119 from Bury St Edmunds via Stowmarket

With its intact cliff of curtain wall and fine views over beautiful Suffolk countryside from its ramparts and towers, most people would probably rank Framlingham as the most impressive castle in East Anglia. Certainly it is one of the most interesting of England's twelfth-century castles, being the earliest recognizable attempt at a 'keepless' castle – the forerunner of the concentric castles of the following century.

As a Norman manor, Framlingham was first granted by Henry I to Roger Bigod in 1100–1. Roger broke with convention by not strengthening the manor with a motte-and-bailey castle. He contented himself instead with a wooden hall surrounded by a palisade and ditch, enclosed by a 'wrap-around' bailey on three sides and an artificial lake on the fourth. Henry II, wanting no rivals to his castle at Orford, ordered Roger's son Hugh Bigod, first Earl

The western walkway at Framlingham, with the ornate twisted decorative chimneys – all that remains of the splendid sixteenth-century Great Hall.

Framlingham's main gate, surmounted by the Howard coat of arms. The 3rd Howard duke rebuilt the gateway between 1525 and 1550.

of Norfolk, to dismantle Framlingham's palisades in 1175; but the second earl, Roger Bigod II, wasted no time in rebuilding Framlingham in stone when Henry II died in 1189. The curtain wall and towers date from this reconstruction.

The Bigods held Framlingham until 1306, when it was taken under Crown control. It was later granted to the Mowbrays, first dukes of Norfolk (1375–1476), and passed to the related Howards; but the third Howard duke, falling foul of Henry VIII, lost Framlingham in forfeiture to the Crown.

The bridge over the moat, leading to the main gate in Framlingham's southern wall. The walkway can be seen through the gap in the battlements to the right.

Henry's son Edward VI gave the castle to his half-sister, Mary, and it was at Framlingham that Mary mustered her supporters before moving on London to oust Lady Jane Grey in 1553. Queen Mary restored Framlingham to the Howards, but by the end of the sixteenth century, after the fourth duke had been executed for treason by Elizabeth (1572), the castle was back in Crown hands. James I again restored Framlingham to the Howards (1613), who sold it to Sir Robert Hitcham in 1635; and Hitcham bequeathed the castle to Pembroke College, Cambridge (1636), on condition that a poor-house be built on the site of the old Great Hall. East Anglia's adherence to the Parliamentarian cause saved Framlingham from Civil War damage; and finally, in 1913, Pembroke College entrusted Framlingham to the nation. It all added up to a highly colourful if non-violent history, preserving a fine set of castle defences virtually intact.

Framlingham's glory is its irregular oval curtain wall and 13 rectangular flanking towers, connected by a walkway open to visitors. Fine 'twisted' chimneys of ornate brick serve as a reminder of the Tudor mansion which the castle became under the Howards. Looking down on the Inner Court from the walkway it is easy to see Framlingham as a forerunner not only of the concentric castles of the thirteenth century, but also of the fortified manors of the fourteenth and fifteenth.

Looking west from Framlingham's walkway towards the lake, with the interior of the ruined Prison Tower in the foreground.

The cliff-like curtain wall and towers of Framlingham,

seen to particularly fine advantage from the west, across the lake.

CASTLE RISING, NORFOLK

Department of the Environment
3 miles (4·8 km) NE King's Lynn; A1078/A149 from King's Lynn;
A149 from Hunstanton; A148 from Fakenham; A47/A149 from Norwich

Castle Rising is a hulking brute of a castle: one of the largest rectangular keeps in the country, with its mass only accentuated by its low height of under 60 feet (18·3 m). It was built by William d'Albini in the mid-twelfth century, later passing to the redoubtable Warennes.

Despite its intimidating strength, the outside walls of this 'great keep' are quite richly decorated with arcading which can have served no military purpose. The first-floor main entrance is protected by a forebuilding reminiscent of the one at Rochester – an anticipation of the later barbican.

The staircase leading to Castle Rising's main gate: how an attacker would have seen it from inside the 'killing bottle' of the forebuilding.

The squat mass of Castle Rising's twelfth-century great keep is graced with decorative stonework, and the main gate screened by a forebuilding.

The generous ground area permitted the incorporation of the castle's domestic amenities – great hall and kitchens, a gallery and a chapel – on only two floors. This was a simple way of achieving a more solid mass and making mining less effective. The castle's outworks were completed on an equally massive scale and can still be traced.

Castle Rising will always be associated with Queen Isabelle of France, Edward III's mother. Having deposed her husband Edward II, and having raised no recorded objection to his appalling murder at Berkeley, Isabelle had governed the country in the name of her son, in collusion with her lover Mortimer (January 1327–October 1329). This state of affairs ended abruptly when Mortimer was toppled by a *coup d'état* headed by the young King, with Mortimer seized in the Queen's chamber and hauled off to London for summary trial and execution. Edward III then gave his mother Castle Rising as her sole remaining estate. Apart from the occasional journey with her son's approval, Isabelle remained at Castle Rising, frequently visited by Edward, until her death there 28 years later in 1358.

A closer look at the extensive stone decorations on the exterior of Castle Rising keep.

NORWICH, NORFOLK

Borough of Norwich

Norwich Castle is another huge, early twelfth-century 'great keep', a massive rectangle of masonry 96 feet by 76 feet (29·3 m by 23·2 m), which replaced the original post-Conquest stockade of 1067 in 1125. The Norwich keep was originally screened by outworks, but whereas those of the White Tower in London continued to expand into the neighbouring city, those at Norwich were devoured by the increasing prosperity of the medieval town. Like Castle Rising, Norwich keep's outer walls are decorated with patterns of blank arcading – carefully restored by the Norwich city fathers in 1833–9.

And yet, as with the great keeps of Rochester, London and Colchester, the strength of Norwich Castle proved of little use during the Peasants'

Looking across Norwich City towards the commanding silhouette of the castle.

Revolt of 1381. Assembling on Mousehold Heath outside Norwich, the rebels led by Geoffrey Litster demanded and got the surrender of both city and castle (17 June 1381). Hailed as 'King of the Commons', Litster feasted in state in the castle while his followers looted the city. But their timing was wrong: the Revolt had already collapsed in the south-east. When the fighting Bishop of Norwich, Henry Despenser, marched on Norwich a week later, Litster and his adherents fled from the city. (They were overtaken at North Walsham, where Litster was solemnly absolved of his sins and hanged without further ado.)

Much the same happened 168 years later during

Blank arcading on the exterior of Norwich Castle, a reminder of the fine work in castle preservation achieved by the city fathers in the nineteenth century.

'Kett's Revolt' (1549) when Robert Kett, a respected local landowner, assumed the leadership of Norfolk peasantry reduced to beggary by the greedy enclosure of common land. Though Norwich city and castle again capitulated to the insurgents, Kett kept his followers in good order, in camp on Mousehold Heath. But it did him little good when they were smashed by German mercenaries hired by the Earl of Warwick. Exempted from pardon, Kett was hanged from the battlements of Norwich Castle – a great-hearted man still remembered in Norfolk with almost a folk-hero's dues.

Norwich Castle is yet another example of the excellent work done by the Victorians in castle preservation. In 1894, having been used for centuries as the city prison, the castle became the city museum instead. Here in the old keep is one of the finest city museums in England, with excellent displays of local archaeological finds, natural history and works of art.

CAISTER, NORFOLK

Privately owned
1 mile (1·6 km) w of Caister-on-Sea;
A1064 from Great Yarmouth;
A47/A1064 from Norwich via Acle

Caister is a fifteenth-century fortified manor in brick, and one of the finest specimens of its kind. Privately owned, it is open to the public from May to September, and a motor museum is one of its many attractions.

The castle belongs to the period when private castle-building under royal licence was rapidly falling off. There had been 52 such licences in the reign of Richard II (1377–99), and 11 in the reigns of Henry IV and Henry V (1399–1422). Under Henry VI (1422–60) there were only five, of which Caister was one. It was built by one of the most famous Lancastrian soldiers, Sir John Fastolf (nothing to do with Shakespeare's Falstaff, with whom any resemblance is not only accidental but unlikely in the extreme), and financed by the immense ransom extorted for the Duc d'Alençon, captured by Fastolf in one of the battles of the Hundred Years War at Verneuil in 1424. Moated and rectangular in plan, Caister was completed with separate summer and winter halls. Its surviving tower originally had no less than five storeys of rooms.

Caister will be familiar to all who have read the 'Paston Letters', that unique record of a remarkable family's life and times in fifteenth-century England. Fastolf may or may not have been related to John Paston, whom he called 'cousin', but he certainly became deeply indebted to Paston's sharpness in business and the law, and bequeathed Caister to Paston in 1457. The Duke of Norfolk coveted the castle for himself and indignantly disputed the will. In 1470 he resorted to direct action, besieging Caister with 3,000 men against 30 when he was supposed to be pacifying the country for the temporarily restored Henry VI. Not surprisingly, the Pastons were evicted, but thanks to their legal acumen and persistence recovered Caister afterwards.

Caister is a classic fifteenth-century defensible home, with large windows for maximum light as well as circular gunports commanding the moat.

OTHER CASTLES TO VISIT

Pleshey, Essex
Classic Norman motte-and-bailey site which never made the transition to stone defences.

Baconsthorpe, Norfolk
Late fifteenth-century fortified manor, considerably marred by quarrying in the seventeenth century.

THE MIDLANDS

BERKHAMSTED, HERTFORDSHIRE

Department of the Environment
M1 from London to Junction 5, then A41 via Watford,
Hemel Hempstead; A355/A416 from Beaconsfield via Chesham;
M10/A41 from St Albans via Hemel Hempstead

Unlike the Romans, who raised a mighty monument to their conquest of Britain (at Richborough in Kent, where its foundations can still be seen), the Normans created no specific memorial to the Conquest of 1066; but if one exists it is to be found at Berkhamsted Castle. For Berkhamsted is where the war of the Conquest ended – where the *Witan*, the lords of Anglo-Saxon England, came out from London to make formal submission to Duke William after his march through southern England from the field of Hastings. The new manor of Berkhamsted was presented by William I to his half-brother Robert of Mortain, who built one of the most ambitious 'first-generation' motte-and-bailey castles to have survived in recognizable form to the present day.

Berkhamsted is a castle where the decay of the later stonework, so far from erasing the entire complex, has left an impressive amount of the original works showing. The castle is a larger than usual motte-and-bailey, with a twelfth-century replacement shell keep on the motte and about half of the bailey curtain wall remaining. But the most remarkable aspect of Berkhamsted's surviving defences is the outer girdle of earthworks and the unique double moat – not only one of the oldest, but easily the most original system of water defences of any English castle.

However, combat experience in Berkhamsted's most dramatic siege proved that the castle's double moat lay too close to the bailey. In the civil war of 1216 a besieging army, well armed with siege catapults, battered down the bailey defences and rendered the castle indefensible in a mere 14 days.

*Berkhamsted's unique
double moat.*

WARWICK, WARWICKSHIRE

Privately owned

Warwick Castle falls into the same category as Bodiam and Tattershall: everyone's ideal of what a medieval castle *should* look like. It has survived unslighted by vandals, unmarred by battle damage, and superbly preserved: a monument to the great Beauchamp earls of Warwick, who raised the castle to its peak of glory in the fourteenth and fifteenth centuries.

As a thriving Old English royal *burh* of the tenth and early eleventh centuries, Warwick was predestined to receive a Norman castle during the Conquest. The first motte-and-bailey was sited there in 1067, safeguarding William I's march to York to cow the northern English earls into submission. The outlines of the original motte and bailey can still be seen. The castle went through the standard transition to stone defences in the twelfth and thirteenth centuries, but its present-day appearance dates from the late fourteenth century, when it was almost completely rebuilt by the Beauchamp earls as both an improved stronghold and a luxury residence.

The residential apartments are in the south range – the Great Hall with its fine collection of armour, the state dining room, and the library. The great towers stand on the north side of the rebuilt bailey, with its gatehouse and barbican flanked by Caesar's Tower and Guy's Tower. These have the pronounced machicolations already mentioned in connection with Nunney, built in the same period. The strength of the castle's fighting north front is sustained by the water defence of the river Avon in front of the residential south side.

Warwick is no mere shell of a once-proud castle: it is a magnificently preserved fortified home, full of interest, to which a brief visit cannot do justice.

Warwick Castle from Castle Bridge : a superb monument to the Beauchamp earls of Warwick, who completely rebuilt it in the late fourteenth century.

BERKELEY, GLOUCESTERSHIRE

Privately owned
From Bristol, M5 to Junction 14, then A38/B4509;
from Gloucester, M5 to Junction 13, then A38/B4066;
from Cirencester, A419 via Stroud to Frampton Severn, then A38/B4066

If Windsor is remarkable as the oldest royal residential castle in England, Berkeley is its counterpart: the oldest residential castle in England to have been held by the same family for the past 800 years. (Berkeley's family tradition is actually a century older than that of Windsor, which really only dates from the rebuilding by Henry III, whereas Berkeley passed to Robert FitzHarding in the reign of Henry II.) Berkeley will probably go on being remembered, however, for the terrible screams heard outside the castle when Edward II was foully murdered there in September 1327. And this is a pity, for here is one of England's most beautiful castles, both in itself and in its countryside setting.

Berkeley is a thirteenth- and fourteenth-century residential rebuilding of an eleventh-century motte-and-bailey founded by William FitzOsbern (died 1071), the steward of Normandy, who was created Earl of Hereford by William I and entrusted with the security of the southern Welsh border zone. The castle's conversion to shell keep and stone curtain wall began under Robert FitzHarding, forebear of

*Enormous barrels in
the vaulted beer
cellar.*

the Berkeley family of today, who received the castle from Henry II in 1154. Like Farnham in Surrey Berkeley's shell keep is a rarity. It was built round the foot of the motte instead of the top, but whereas Farnham's shell keep was filled in to create a solid drum, that of Berkeley was subsequently excavated,

*Berkeley Castle, a stronghold and residence with an unbroken history of family residence
dating back 800 years.*

One of Berkeley's magnificent drawing rooms, known as the Long Drawing Room to distinguish it from the Small Drawing Room.

Berkeley's main gate, surmounted by the family arms, placed in a tower facing the inner courtyard.

with the motte entirely removed to create a circular courtyard.

Berkeley's keep contains the famous room where Edward II was imprisoned and eventually murdered after his deposition in 1327 – a crime which, as the castle guide-book carefully explains, was none of the Berkeley family's doing. It looks rather nice today, with interesting furniture and plenty of light admitted through snug-looking windows, but its present-day look is that created by the rebuilding of Berkeley in 1340–50. By all accounts Edward was penned in a cell made noisome by the cesspit below, into which rotting carcasses were thrown in hopes that the fumes would kill him off. The agents of Mortimer and Queen Isabelle were disappointed, however, for Edward was physically very tough and survived. In the end, the story goes, he was overpowered in the night, pinned down and had his bowels burned out with a red-hot poker 'putte thro the secret place posterialle'.

None of this notoriety, however, can detract from the beauty and grandeur of Berkeley: one of England's best-preserved castles, a living achievement by a remarkable family to whom we owe a great debt of gratitude.

GOODRICH, HEREFORD & WORCESTER

Department of the Environment
M5/M50 to Ross-on-Wye;
A40 from Ross-on-Wye, Monmouth

A stronghold of the Welsh frontier, Goodrich Castle still crowns the skyline, blocking the crossing of the River Wye.

A frontier fortress from its origin, reaching its peak strength in the Welsh wars of Edward I, Goodrich is an excellent model of castle evolution, from the tower keep of the eleventh and twelfth centuries to the concentric castle defences of the thirteenth. What makes this castle really impressive, however, is its dramatic site: crowning the heights above the river Wye, the old frontier between Norman England and the fiercely independent principality of Wales.

Goodrich Castle gets its name from 'Godric's Castle', the Godric in question being Godric Mappestone, who built the first Norman stronghold there at the close of the eleventh century. This can still be seen at the core of Goodrich's defences: a small, square tower keep of three storeys. In the

reign of King John, Goodrich passed to one of the greatest warriors of the age, loyal servant to Henry II, Richard I, John and the young Henry III: William the Marshal, the 'Good Knight', and arguably the inspiration for the Sir Lancelot in medieval romance. The Marshal gave Goodrich an ambitious curtain wall outside the west and north sides, extended by a dry ditch to the east and south.

From about 1280, however, during the decisive conquest of Wales by Edward I, the King's uncle William de Valence rebuilt Goodrich again as a square, concentric castle on an entirely new plan. The original tower keep was now enclosed on the south side of a central courtyard. Thrusting out from the corners of the outer curtain were four cylindrical flanking towers, each flaring out at the foot into a solid battered square base. Each of these towers was designed as a fortress in itself. It would have been useless for an attacker to storm or breach the curtain wall (assuming such a feat were possible); every tower would have to be taken in turn. The result was one of the strongest English castles of the age.

Three and a half centuries were to pass before

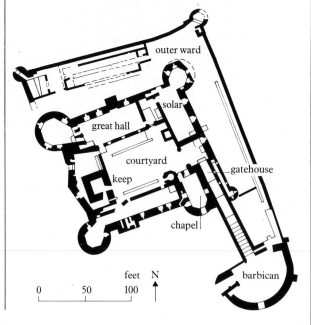

The private apartments: the floor level of the upper-storey solar can be traced on the wall to the right; to the left is the well-head.

Goodrich's mighty walls met the fire-power of modern artillery, which the castle was unable to mount itself. Twice besieged in the Civil War, the castle held out valiantly for King Charles in 1646, commanded by Sir Henry Lingen, until the south walls were breached by a Parliamentarian siege gun by the name of 'Roaring Meg'. (She is still to be seen beside Hereford Cathedral, on Castle Green.) Even after 'Roaring Meg's' depredations, Lingen's garrison fought on until the Parliamentarians captured the well-head and cut off the defenders' water supply. But even Parliamentarian battle damage and post-war slighting and quarrying could not detract from what Wordsworth, a regular visitor to the Wye valley, was to call 'the noblest ruin in Herefordshire'.

DUDLEY, WEST MIDLANDS

Borough of Dudley
9 miles (14·5 km) w of Birmingham

With the best will in the world, it is hard to imagine Dudley Castle as it was in its fourteenth-century heyday, for modern Dudley is the 'Capital of the Black Country', hemmed in on all sides by industrial sprawl. This is where coal started to be used for smelting iron in the seventeenth century, with hideous results for the landscape. It has been said of Dudley that no fewer than seven counties could be seen from the castle's Norman keep – air pollution permitting. The Clean Air Acts, however, have wrought miracles over the past 20 years, and Dudley is still an excellent place for a family visit because it has a zoo: an appropriate attraction for a castle, as it is consistent with medieval tradition (even the Tower of London once had its zoo, in the now-vanished Lion Tower).

The first Dudley Castle was a post-Conquest motte-and-bailey, but this was destroyed on Henry II's orders in 1174 when its overlord, Roger de Mowbray, unwisely backed the rebellion of Henry 'The Young King' and the invading Scots. The new castle was that decided rarity, a tower keep on a motte, proving the natural firmness of the site. By 1324 Dudley had developed into a sufficiently important castle to be coveted by Edward II's popularly hated favourite, Hugh Despenser. He got his hands on Dudley by the simple expedient of keeping the rightful owner, John de Sutton, in prison until the castle was handed over.

Dudley stands on an imposing limestone bluff, and the 200-foot (61-m) slopes below the castle are served by a chair-lift. The Norman keep is screened by extensive fourteenth-century outer defences, with a courtyard surrounded by a massive curtain wall. Two drum towers and a fine barbican survived a Civil War siege in 1644 and the Parliamentarian slighting that followed in 1646; and further damage was caused by a bad fire in 1750. This was the only important castle of its type in the old county of Worcestershire.

Dudley Castle
from the air.

TATTERSHALL, LINCOLNSHIRE

National Trust
12 miles (19·3 km) NE of Sleaford, A153

To describe the magnificent castle at Tattershall, which at first sight looks like a giant tower keep, as a mere 'fortified manor' seems almost ludicrously inadequate; but this is in fact the most accurate definition. This soaring masterpiece in brick was

The great brick tower of Tattershall, built by the 3rd Lord Cromwell in 1434–45, seen from the south-east.

The beautiful brick-vaulted gallery at Tattershall, with heraldic bosses bearing the arms of (from front to back) Tateshale, Deincourt, and Cromwell.

built in 1434–45 by Ralph, 3rd Baron Cromwell, who was Treasurer of England under Henry VI from 1433 to 1443. Later it passed to the Earls of Lincoln from 1573 to 1693, after which it lay unoccupied until American speculators began shipping it piecemeal to the United States in 1910. Lord Curzon, saviour of Bodiam, thereupon intervened, bought Tattershall himself and restored it, with its outer defences, to its former glory. The castle was bequeathed to the National Trust in 1925.

Lord Curzon's extensive excavations during the restoration of Tattershall revealed the foundations of the original stone castle, built in 1231 by Ralph de Tateshale, after whom the manor was named. But the restoration work also revealed the outer defences which Cromwell had added: an inner ward ringed by a bank and moat, and an outer ward ringed by a second bank, a second moat and yet a third bank. The great tower itself has four storeys (plus an enormous basement area), the fourth storey consisting of a covered gallery below roof level with a parapet walk above. The 'great chamber' on the second storey, above the first-storey 'great hall', doubled as sitting-room and bedroom for the lord of the castle; the entire third storey seems to have been set aside for the women of the household.

At Tattershall, therefore, we find the wheel turned full circle from the dark and comfortless tower keeps of the eleventh and twelfth centuries: all the virtues of strength, increased by concentric outer defences, are combined here with the luxury of any orthodox great house of the period.

LINCOLN, LINCOLNSHIRE

Borough of Lincoln

Cobb Hall, the two-storey dungeon tower in the north-eastern angle of Lincoln's curtain wall, where executions were carried out until 1859.

Before the frontier of Roman Britain was pushed north to the line of Hadrian's Wall, Lincoln had been the base of the 9th Legion: a walled legionary fortress. Some nine centuries later the walls of Roman Lincoln were still recognizable (if not fully defensible) at the time of the Norman Conquest.

Wishing in 1068 to site a particularly strong castle at Lincoln, William I ordered the building of a 'hermit-crab' motte-and-bailey, using the south-west corner of the old Roman walls. The motte and keep were not enclosed by the bailey, but instead were incorporated a third of the way along the southern bailey wall. The area of the bailey (still known as the Bail) was extensive: Domesday Book recorded that no fewer than 166 houses were swept away during the building of the castle. The conversion to stone in the twelfth century produced a shell keep – the Lucy Tower – on the motte, incorporated in a now-formidable walled perimeter. The castle originally had two gateways, one in the west and the other in the east. The western gateway was subsequently blocked, but can still be seen, delineated by a massive Norman arch; the eastern gateway was retained as the main castle entrance, transformed by a massive twin-tower gatehouse in the fourteenth century. This followed on from the thirteenth-century addition of a two-storey flanking tower, Cobb Hall, at the castle's north-eastern corner. Though loopholed for defence it was used as a jail – the iron rings for securing prisoners to the walls are still there – and as an execution chamber as late as 1859.

Lincoln Castle's finest hour was in the civil war of 1216–17, when it represented the high-water mark of the French Prince Louis' ambitions in England. The castle was resolutely defended for the boy king Henry III by a gallant old lady: Nicolaa de la Haye, the widowed holder of Lincoln's hereditary constableship. She held on at Lincoln until a relieving army, commanded by the aged veteran, William the Marshal, arrived on the scene. While the Marshal's forces drove the surprised French into the confines of the city, Nicolaa's garrison sortied to catch the invaders between hammer and anvil – a victory so easy that the triumphant English remembered it as the 'Fair of Lincoln' (20 May 1217).

The English Civil War, however, yielded no such glory. On 6 May 1644, Lincoln Castle was stormed by Parliamentarian forces using the most basic of tactics: escalade, a rush to the walls with storming-ladders. As soon as the Parliamentarians gained the wall the Royalists turned and ran, and the castle fell. For this Charles II had only himself to blame. Eager for any method of raising revenue without calling Parliament, he had sold off the land traversed by the defensive ditch outside the wall, on which houses had subsequently been built. This made it all the easier for his enemies to gain the foot of the wall and capture what had formerly been one of the strongest city castles in the land.

ASHBY-DE-LA-ZOUCH, LEICESTERSHIRE

Department of the Environment
A50 from Leicester via Coalville and Burton-upon-Trent;
A512 from Loughborough; A453 from Nottingham

Ashby-de-la-Zouch is most famous as the scene of the great tournament in Sir Walter Scott's *Ivanhoe*, at which the champions of the scheming Prince John are put to shame by the loyal Ivanhoe and Locksley the archer. Scott, however, seems to have picked on Ashby more for its swashbuckling name than for any real historical connection with the early 1190s, when it was still an unremarkable Norman manor. In the twelfth century the manor was held by the Zouch family, who named it after their home in Brittany. It was probably little more than a walled manor in the mid-fifteenth century, when the huge kitchen was added.

Ashby only attained real prominence after 1461, when Edward IV granted it to the Hastings family. It was Lord Hastings who added the splendid tower, which still survives, along with parts of the walls and solar, which has a fine fireplace and ornate mullioned windows. Under the command of Henry Hastings, Lord Loughborough, Ashby received the defeated King Charles after Naseby (June 1645), and later held out for the King in a siege lasting over a year. This achievement, however, literally brought about Ashby's ruin: an extensive slighting which this fortified manor, with the exception of the tower, could not withstand.

The remains of the tower residence at Ashby-de-la-Zouch. Stronger than Tattershall tower, it was built by Lord Hastings in the reign of Edward IV.

NEWARK, NOTTINGHAMSHIRE

Borough of Newark
A1 from Grantham, Worksop;
A46 from Lincoln, Leicester

Newark Castle is one of the most savagely slighted victims of the English Civil War, in which it served as the main Royalist stronghold in the north-east Midlands from December 1643 to May 1646. Assigned to the bishopric of Lincoln in the post-Conquest settlement, the original motte-and-bailey castle of Newark was rebuilt as a stone tower by Bishop Alexander in 1125. After 1139, when the castle passed to the Crown, the huge and elaborate north gatehouse was added, followed by the south-west corner turret and the extensive crypt, with eight bays.

Like Corfe, Newark was a favourite castle of King John, who withdrew there to die in October 1216. In the civil war which ensued, Newark was garrisoned and held for the boy king Henry III by John's mercenaries; in the following year, it served as the advanced base for William the Marshal's brilliant relief of Lincoln Castle.

In the fourteenth and fifteenth centuries the castle was modified as a residence, the great hall being lit by three large windows in the west wall, and two towers added to the corners of the same wall.

In the Civil War, after Newark had been captured by Royalist cavalry in December 1643, it was a thorn in the side of the Parliamentarian cause for two and a half years, constantly inhibiting Parliamentarian strategy with the threat of a Royalist advance into the Parliamentarian heartland of East Anglia. It was half-heartedly besieged in March 1644, the year of the Parliamentary victory at Marston Moor, but the garrison was speedily relieved by Prince Rupert. The final siege was begun in November 1645, when the Parliamentarians were aided by a Scots Presbyterian expeditionary force. The garrison commander, Lord Bellasis, surrendered on the King's orders in May 1646. He and his men were granted the honours of war, but the ensuing slighting left only the west side of the castle standing – a viciously mutilated yet still imposing ruin.

Newark Castle, where King John withdrew to die in 1216. Having been held for Charles I in the Civil War, it was mercilessly slighted by the Parliamentarians.

PEVERIL, DERBYSHIRE

Department of the Environment
A625, Sheffield/Castleton; A6/A625, Manchester/
Stockport/New Mills/Whaley Bridge/Castleton

Midway between the modern conurbations of Manchester to the west and Sheffield to the east, Peveril is another castle well-known to fans of Sir Walter Scott, with a starring role in *Peveril of the Peak*. It was always a castle of limited national importance by virtue of its small size and isolation, but it was nevertheless an essential possession for any lord wanting to control the central Peak District and its lead mines.

Peveril is worth the long climb to reach its eyrie-like triangular site, protected on two sides by sheer crags (the south-east side has no wall) and to the northern front – the longer side of the triangle – by steep slopes dropping away to the road. Apart from the amazing views it offers, Peveril is interesting because it is one of the handful of eleventh-century stone castles built, from its beginnings, with a curtain wall. The western and northern walls also have small projecting turrets to permit a measure of lateral fire along the foot of the wall.

Peveril's curtain wall was built by William Peveril in 1090; but its small square keep is a later addition (1176). This was too small to accommodate a garrison in anything like comfort, and traces of a modest hall have been found close to the keep.

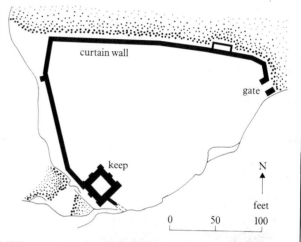

Peveril Castle, one of the very few eleventh-century castles with a stone curtain wall.

BEESTON, CHESHIRE

Department of the Environment
A51/A49 from Chester and Crewe

Beeston Castle stands on an immense crag 500 feet (152 m) high – one of the most daunting natural castle sites anywhere in England. It was always a stronghold pure and simple, and could never have evolved into a residential and administrative centre like Ludlow. One of the most impressive sections of the defences is the frowning pair of semicircular towers flanking the gateway. Among its most pressing problems, however, was that of the water supply, as indicated by the prodigious depth (370 feet/113 m) of the well shaft.

Beeston was built by Ranulf de Blundeville, Earl of Chester, who died in 1232. It was later occupied by Simon de Montfort, and served as a refuge for those of his followers who managed to escape the defeat of de Montfort's army at Evesham in 1265. Later, according to popular belief, Richard II, hastening back from Ireland in 1399 to meet the invasion of his usurping cousin Henry of Bolingbroke (afterwards Henry IV), buried his treasure at Beeston before falling into his enemies' hands. The castle's ruinous condition is due to Parliamentarian slighting after the Civil War – no doubt carried out all the more viciously because Beeston had been the scene of a humiliating Parliamentarian defeat, when a 'forlorn hope' storming party of eight Royalists managed to scale the north wall and bluff the 80-strong garrison into surrender. Beeston then remained in Royalist hands for two years before being blockaded into surrender.

The massive twin towers of Beeston's gatehouse. The castle was the scene of a daring Royalist assault in the English Civil War.

ACTON BURNELL, SHROPSHIRE

Department of the Environment
A458 from Shrewsbury, direction Much Wenlock;
turn right at Cross Houses for Pitchford and Acton Burnell

Acton Burnell is not the easiest castle to find; though only 4 miles (6·5 km) from Shrewsbury, it is tucked away south of the Shrewsbury/Bridgnorth road (but clearly marked on the Ordnance Survey map of the region). It is well worth the effort, however: one of the earliest fortified manor houses in England, and one of the most intact, it stands, beautifully kept, amid lawns and overshadowed by a giant cedar. It is a charming, red sandstone building with a tower at each end, and only the roof missing. Try to pick a sunny day, when the sandstone is seen to best advantage.

Acton Burnell owes its second name ('Acton' means a forest clearing) to Roger Burnell, a favourite clerical civil servant of Edward I who became first Chancellor of England and later Bishop of Bath and Wells. Though Edward I failed to negotiate Burnell's appointment as Archbishop of Canterbury (perhaps this was just as well, given the tragic experience of Henry II and *his* friend Becket in the previous century) he did grant him this

Acton Burnell, one of the earliest English fortified manors, shaded by a giant cedar tree.

Shropshire manor in 1284. A lucrative perquisite accompanying the grant was permission to cut timber in the royal forests of Shropshire. The house was completed in 1293 and remained in the Bishop's family until 1420, when it was abandoned.

The courtyard of Acton Burnell, rebuilt as a residence for Bishop Burnell in the reign of Edward I, showing generous windows and capacious chambers.

STOKESAY, SHROPSHIRE

Privately owned
A49, Ludlow/Shrewsbury; 6 miles (9·6 km) NW of Ludlow

Stokesay ranks with Acton Burnell as one of the earliest English fortified manor houses, being of late thirteenth-century vintage. Its unique appearance makes it one of the best-known smaller English castles, but its supreme value is that it offers a perfect example of what the long-vanished domestic interiors of larger castles would have looked like 600 years ago.

The castle was begun by the Say family in about 1240, but was bought in 1280 by Laurence de Ludlow, a rich wool merchant, who received Edward I's licence to crenellate about ten years later. Laurence completed the hall with its two squat flanking towers, adding a curtain wall and encircling moat. The Ludlow family retained the castle for 300 years before selling it in the early sixteenth century, and later owners added the splendid timbered gatehouse into the courtyard.

Stokesay is a chameleon: it looks completely different from the changing viewpoints as you walk round it. From the north, the walls and tower at the far end look formidable; from the west, the half-timbered residential upper storeys look welcoming and comfortable. Stokesay is indeed the epitome of the *domus defensabilis*, the 'defensible home'. It has a pitched and tiled roof, and amazingly large windows for so early a fortification. The fine solar chamber above the Great Hall can only be reached by an outside staircase, giving the solar's inhabitants complete privacy from the bustle in the hall below – which, however, they could observe at will through

Rich carving on the timbers of the Elizabethan tower gatehouse which commands the courtyard.

The finely timbered Great Hall at Stokesay: on the right is the doorway to the courtyard, and the stairs at the far end lead to the half-timbered north tower chamber.

'squint' windows on either side of the magnificent fireplace. A half-timbered upper storey, sprouting from the north tower, provided the family and their guests with additional accommodation. At the other end of the castle, the south tower, reached by a drawbridge connecting it with the solar, was clearly Stokesay's 'survival shelter' for extreme emergency.

In the Civil War Stokesay's owner, Lord Craven, garrisoned the castle as a northern outpost for Ludlow, but happily Stokesay surrendered without firing a shot – and so was saved from Parliamentarian slighting. Thus was preserved one of the most attractive of all 'time-capsules' of medieval castle life.

Stokesay from the north, with the incongruous but appealing half-timbered chamber projecting from the north tower.

LUDLOW, SHROPSHIRE

Borough of Ludlow
A4117 from Kidderminster;
A44/A49 from Worcester via Leominster;
A49 from Hereford, Shrewsbury

During the extensive reconstruction of about 1330 this four-storey tower crowned with a hexagonal turret was built into the angle of the outer wall.

Fifteen miles (24·1 km) south-west of Bridgnorth, Ludlow was one of England's greatest fighting castles and the most impressive stronghold on the Welsh March. Like nearly all its fellow castles on the Welsh frontier, Ludlow boasts extensive stone defences dating from the eleventh century, the period of the first curtain-wall defences in English castle-building. The castle was founded in 1085 by Roger de Lacy, on rising ground enclosed by the junction of the Corve and Teme rivers.

The layout chosen by de Lacy for his new castle was both audacious and novel. The audacity was the sheer size of it: the outer bailey could comfortably accommodate a cricket match, while the inner bailey annually houses both actors and audience for the Shakespearian productions of the Ludlow Summer Festival. The novelty was his modification of traditional castle design. Ludlow's layout derived from the familiar interlock of inner and outer baileys, with the inner bailey in the north-west corner of the outer perimeter; but there was no distinct keep as such, either on a motte or in the form of a great tower. The nearest equivalent at Ludlow is the square tower guarding the entrance to the inner bailey – clearly a forerunner of the great tower gatehouses of the coming two centuries. As at

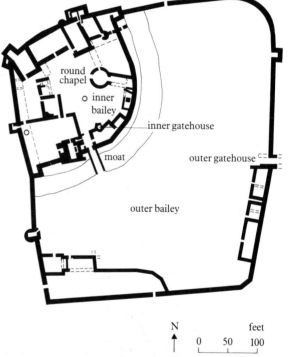

smaller castles of the same period, like Peveril, Ludlow's outer wall is studded with projecting square towers.

Another startling novelty, unique to Ludlow, is the chapel projecting into the inner bailey, anchored to the bailey wall. The west end of the chapel's nave swells into a cylindrical tower, another potential addition to the castle's innermost defences.

Ludlow's role was never restricted to that of a military stronghold: it was a centre of royal administration, the seat not only of the Mortimer Earls of March and subsequently of the House of York, but also of the Lords President of the Council of the Marches – an office which endured until its abolition by Oliver Cromwell. For the latter reason alone, quite apart from the natural capacity of the castle precincts, Ludlow received a steady succession of residential buildings, culminating in the sixteenth-century Great Hall – the evolution of a Norman stronghold into a Tudor palace.

Unlike most other English castles, Ludlow played an active part in both the Wars of the Roses and the Civil War. In the former it was a Yorkist stronghold, and from Ludlow in 1483 the young Edward v was conducted to London – ostensibly for his coronation, in reality to meet an unknown fate with his younger brother in the Tower. Though subjected to slighting for its adherence to the Royalist cause in the Civil War, Ludlow's defences were far too massive to be razed.

This is one of the foremost English castles: a superb and inspiring specimen of medieval military architecture, built to secure a conquest, and developed as a seat of government.

Zig-zag ornamentation crowning the Norman doorway to the round chapel at Ludlow.

The fortifications of Ludlow, built by Roger de Lacy to a novel and audacious design.

The inner bailey at Ludlow, showing the round

BRIDGNORTH, SHROPSHIRE

Borough of Bridgnorth
A454 from Wolverhampton; A422 from Telford;
A458 from Shrewsbury; A442 from Kidderminster

Standing 100 feet (30 m) above the river Severn, Bridgnorth is perhaps most famous for being one of Britain's three noted 'leaning tower' castles: a giant section of early medieval masonry has been leaning at an apparently impossible angle ever since the Parliamentarians slighted the castle after the Civil War. The other two are Caerphilly in Wales and Bramber in Sussex.

Bridgnorth commands one of the most strategic crossings on the upper Severn; there had been a Saxon *burh* there since 912. The castle was built in 1101 by the notorious Earl of Shrewsbury, Robert de Bellême, whose extensive holdings in England and Normandy included Arundel, as he was the Montgomery heir. Earl Robert has the unenviable reputation of having been the worst of the Norman barons: a vicious sadist who would much rather torture prisoners than ransom them, and whose wife (married, of course, for her lands) spent most of her married life in a dungeon at Bellême. He rebelled against Henry I in 1102, but the King promptly took the field and captured all of Earl Robert's castles, including Arundel and Bridgnorth. Henry finally imprisoned Earl Robert for life in 1112.

Troublesome subject though he was, Earl Robert was nevertheless a fine military architect whose keep at Bridgnorth was generally regarded as impossible to take except by blockade and starvation. It served England well as a 'frontier castle' on the Welsh March throughout the twelfth and thirteenth centuries, and again in the Glendower revolt of the early fourteenth. Its last siege was against the Parliamentarians in the Civil War, when it remained defiant even after the extensive slighting of 1646. The 30-foot (9·1-m) slab of the tower which refused to collapse has remained ever since at an almost incredible angle of 17 degrees from the vertical – over three times the 'lean' of the leaning tower of Pisa.

OTHER CASTLES TO VISIT

Astley, Warwickshire
Sixteenth-century fortified manor with twelfth-century moat and outer walls. Lady Jane Grey lived here. Serves today as a noted restaurant.

Kenilworth, Warwickshire
Glorious Tudor castle-into-mansion, with twelfth-century keep and fourteenth-century Great Hall.

Thornbury, Gloucestershire
One of the last defensible manor houses built in England, by the Duke of Buckingham in 1511. Now a fine restaurant (advance bookings required).

Broughton, Oxfordshire
Tudor mansion rebuilt from fourteenth-century fortified manor, with early fifteenth-century gate-house and wide moat. Superb Tudor plaster ceiling in original Great Hall.

Belvoir (pron. 'Beever'), **Leicestershire**
Famous castle-mansion of original eleventh-century foundation, repeatedly rebuilt. Present appearance mostly from eighteenth- and nineteenth-century reconstructions.

Kirby Muxloe, Leicestershire
Moated brick fortified manor house of late fifteenth century (1480–4), begun by the Lord Hastings executed by Richard III. Appropriately lies about 8 miles (12·9 km) from the battlefield of Bosworth where Richard III was killed.

Nottingham, Nottinghamshire
City museum and art gallery, housed in seventeenth- and eighteenth-century rebuilding of renowned castle originally founded by William Peveril in 1070. Castle Rock is honeycombed with tunnels and passages, most notably 'Mortimer's Hole', reputedly used for the *coup d'état* which overthrew Edward II's murderer in 1329.

Dalton, Lancashire
Good example of rectangular fourteenth-century peel tower.

Lancaster, Lancashire
Fine twelfth-century keep, with (heavily reconstructed) King John's Hadrian's Tower and gate-house. *Note*: Public access limited to times when castle is not being used as a court-house.

THE NORTH COUNTRY

CONISBROUGH, SOUTH YORKSHIRE

Department of the Environment
A630 from Doncaster, Rotherham

Conisbrough Castle stands on high ground looking down to the river Don, with its 90-foot (27·4-m) white tower keep visible for miles against the surrounding green. It is slightly later than the similar keep at Orford (p. 85), having been built by Hameline de Warenne in about 1185. And whereas Orford keep now stands alone, considerable sections of Conisbrough's outer defences remain.

The main difference between Conisbrough and Orford keeps, both superb examples of their period, is that Conisbrough has six external buttresses to Orford's much thicker three. Again, Conisbrough keep is cylindrical within and without, while the exterior of Orford is polygonal. Apart from the intact keep and sections of the curtain wall, the most impressive surviving part of Conisbrough's defences is the lower section of the gatehouse. The narrow barbican outside is designed with a double angle to deny attackers a direct approach to the gate.

Conisbrough, like Ashby-de-la-Zouch, has connections with *Ivanhoe*, namely the small chapel built into the buttress on the third storey. The roof is still a superb viewpoint, even if some visitors find the modern industrial vista less than inspiring.

The six intact flanking towers of Conisbrough's white stone tower stand in stark contrast to the ruined outerworks.

BOLTON, NORTH YORKSHIRE

Privately owned
4 miles (6·4 km) NW of Middleham,
A6108/A684 via Leyburn

Though Castle Bolton is not the most accessible of North Yorkshire villages, the castle which gave the village its name is worth the trip, and so is its view of Wensleydale.

Bolton is a fortified manor house which has belonged to the Scrope family for 600 years. The first Lord Scrope obtained his licence to crenellate in 1379, the second year of Richard II's reign, and rather than reconstruct his existing manor house (the usual practice) he built an entirely new one. Only half of this is in use today, the other half having been ruined in the Civil War.

The new castle placed the emphasis firmly on domesticity and comfort, as is apparent from the size of the rooms, and of the windows and fireplaces. The building of chimneys to avoid smoky rooms (part and parcel of domestic life since the Dark Ages) was still a novelty in the late fourteenth century. The castle's four corner towers were used as domestic quarters, with other accommodation grouped round the courtyard. One of the corner towers collapsed in a storm in 1761.

The comfort and space of Bolton was considered fit for the imprisoned Mary, Queen of Scots, in 1568–9. She was confined at Bolton for six months at the start of her 19-year imprisonment in England. The castle's defences, however, were still strong enough to require its garrison to be starved out in the Civil War.

A notable attraction at Bolton is the Wensleydale folk museum in the Great Chamber, and there is also a restaurant.

Bolton Castle, a fine example of a late fourteenth-century fortified manor house, with three of its corner towers still standing.

RICHMOND, NORTH YORKSHIRE

Department of the Environment
A1/A6108 from Darlington via Scotch Corner;
A684/A1/A6136 from Northallerton

Richmond Castle is remarkable for the high proportion of its stone defences dating from the first 20 years after the Norman Conquest, when it was built by a Breton baron, Alan de Ponthièvre. Like many castles in the Midlands and North Country, it was never an earthwork motte-and-bailey, but instead was built from the abundant local stone to exploit a suitable platform of high ground. Such sites naturally dictated the outline of the defences, whether circular, oval or rectangular, but Richmond is a decided novelty: an equilateral triangle, with the castle's fine tower keep and main gateway at the north-eastern apex. Richmond also boasts the oldest castle Great Hall in England (Scolland's Hall, at the southern apex).

The expansion of the original castle began under Henry II in the later twelfth century with the building of the imposing 100-foot (30·5-m) tower keep, entered in the usual fashion by a staircase leading to the first storey. The battlements were repaired (fairly accurately it would seem from other towers of similar type) in the eighteenth century; and the corner turrets have two storeys. But attempts of the same date to provide Richmond with outer defences reveal the limitations of twelfth-century defence works, which concentrated on

A view of Richmond's slighted curtain wall from the south-west, across the river Swale.

The unique triangular plan of Richmond Castle, with the tower keep at the northern apex and the clumsy outer bailey tacked on at right.

strengthening the corners of the original structure. This could not work with a triangular inner perimeter, because the resulting outerworks extended away from each other instead of meshing together. A barbican was built to protect the main entrance beside the keep, and a truncated oval outer ward, the Cock Pit, was extended outward from the southern or Gold Hole Tower. The result was a yawning gap between the barbican's east wall and the eastern angle of the Cock Pit. A clumsy attempt was made to seal this gap with an outer curtain wall, which would have been virtually impossible to defend.

It may seem surprising that a castle as impressive as Richmond had such an uneventful history. Richmond lay well away from the principal lines of communication in medieval times: it commands little but the entrance to Swaledale, which evidently was quite enough for Alan de Ponthièvre.

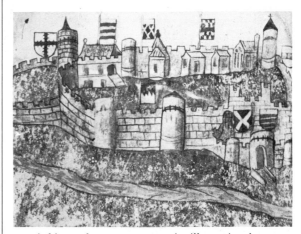

A thirteenth-century manuscript illustration shows Richmond's battlements flaunting heraldic banners, with the keep and barbican shown clearly on the right.

SCARBOROUGH, NORTH YORKSHIRE

Department of the Environment

Seen from the town and harbour, Scarborough Castle looks truly impregnable: a mighty curtain wall studded with eight towers running across the entire horizon of Castle Hill, with the summit of a great tower rising beyond. From each extremity of this daunting barrier, outer walls and defence-works snake menacingly down from the heights.

Nor is this impression deceptive. Though many times besieged, and no less vulnerable to blockade and starvation than any other castle, Scarborough was only once captured by force: in 1645, during the first of two desperate sieges in the English Civil War.

No trace has survived of the first castle built at Scarborough, an adulterine castle, built by William le Gros during the Anarchy of King Stephen's reign in the early twelfth century. Henry II pulled this down and replaced it with a tower keep enclosed by a small bailey. The breathtaking long curtain wall running clean across the headland may have been begun by King John in the early thirteenth century but was certainly completed, with its barbican, under Henry III and Edward I.

As might be expected of a castle on such an

The eastern wall of Scarborough Castle keep : the only wall left intact after the terrible battering taken by the defences in the two sieges of the English Civil War.

exposed site, Scarborough was expensive to maintain. Repair estimates for the year 1619 were for a minimum of £4,000. Its position made it a key strongpoint of the North, however, vital to both sides in the Civil War. At the outset Scarborough was garrisoned for Parliament with a regiment of foot recruited and commanded by a local Member of Parliament, Sir Hugh Cholmley. Always unhappy with the legality of taking up arms against the King, he abandoned the Parliamentarian cause after the first big Royalist victory at Edgehill (October 1642), offering his men the choice either of leaving or of staying as a Royalist garrison. Nearly all stayed for the inevitable Parliamentarian siege, which finally came after the Royalist defeat at Marston Moor in July 1644.

With Parliamentarian outposts only 6 miles away, Cholmley spun out sham surrender negotiations for the next five months, enabling him to get in local supplies and fortify Scarborough town and harbour, on which his chances of receiving seaborne replenishment ultimately depended. When the attack finally began in January 1645 it was made by Parliament's allied Scottish troops, 3,000 in all against Cholmley's 200. By February the Scots had forced the garrison back into the castle and begun an intense bombardment which finally brought down the west side of the keep. Desperate fighting ensued for possession of the gatehouse, in which the Scottish commander was killed; but the attack was renewed under Sir Matthew Boynton, and by July Cholmley's position was hopeless. Those of his men able to walk marched out with the full honours of war on 25 July. Instead of slighting the castle, Parliament voted a day of thanksgiving and £5,000 to repair it. But the victors reckoned without the renewed outbreak of hostilities in 1648, and were always in arrears for payment of their troops. Boynton's son Matthew was now Governor of Scarborough, and he followed Cholmley's example and defected to the Royalist cause. The result was a second siege, hardly less intense than the first, lasting from September to December 1648. Fortunately, the Commonwealth's order for the destruction of the surviving defences of this fine castle was never carried out.

Scarborough's ruined barbican (foreground), with the curtain wall snaking away across the headland to the right and the keep's shattered interior on the skyline.

SKIPTON, NORTH YORKSHIRE

Skipton Castle Ltd
A650/A629 from Bradford via Keighley;
A65 from Leeds via Ilkley;
A56/A59 from Burnley via Nelson and Barrowford;
A59 from Harrogate

There are few more pleasant gateways to the Yorkshire Dales than Skipton, one of the happiest marriages between an unusually attractive country town and the Industrial Revolution. The town's development did not erase the original close association of the castle and Holy Trinity Church as the main focal points at the upper end of the High Street; there are few better examples of a modern town still dominated by its medieval castle.

Only one gateway has survived of the original castle, built in the twelfth century by Robert de Romille to command this valley junction on the upper Aire. The castle passed to the Clifford family in the fourteenth century and was completely rebuilt, receiving a fine curtain wall with rounded towers and a magnificent gatehouse.

What you see today is an object lesson in castle preservation, individual and corporate, dating back over three centuries. Skipton is one of the very few castles to have had the scars of Civil War damage promptly erased after the Restoration of 1660. After serving as a rallying-point for the Royalist forces beaten at Marston Moor in July 1644, Skipton's garrison under Colonel Sir John Mallory fought off its Parliamentarian besiegers until December 1645, and was heavily damaged in the process. Returning to her inheritance after the war, Lady Anne Clifford completely restored not only the castle but also Holy Trinity Church. Lady Anne signed her work by building the family motto into the balustrade over the gatehouse: DESORMAIS – 'Henceforth'. Today the castle is maintained by Skipton Castle Trust, and has an excellent illustrated guide.

Skipton Castle gatehouse with the Clifford family motto, DESORMAIS, built into the balustrade.

PICKERING, NORTH YORKSHIRE

Department of the Environment
A170 from Scarborough; A64/A169 from York via Malton;
A169 from Whitby

*The motte and keep of Pickering Castle, seen from the
'wrap-around' outer bailey which served
as a barbican.*

In total contrast to Helmsley, Pickering is a late eleventh-century motte-and-bailey castle, with stone defences added over the ensuing three centuries. Pickering is a 'two-bailey' castle with a northern inner ward, the shell keep on its motte in the middle, and a southern or outer ward enclosing keep and motte. When the outer ward was given its curtain wall in the fourteenth century, the resulting enclosure served as an enormous encircling barbican for the rest of the castle.

The date of the first castle built at Pickering is obscure, but it seems to have been in the reign of Henry I, early in the twelfth century. It was certainly a royal castle by the latter years of Henry II's reign, when the inner ward's stone curtain wall was built, together with the square Coleman Tower beside the entrance. The castle seems to have suffered heavily in the civil war of 1216–17, because an official enquiry was ordered in 1220 to determine the extent of the damage. The sequel to this enquiry was the rebuilding of the keep as a shell early in the reign of Henry III.

The conversion of the outer ward dates from late in the reign of Edward II and was prompted by a Scottish invasion of the North in the autumn of 1322. The following year Edward visited Pickering and detailed orders were issued for the rebuilding of the outer ward as a stone barbican. This seems to have been completed, with the square flanking towers – Mill Tower, Diate Hill Tower and Rosamund's Tower – by 1326, when Pickering passed to the Duchy of Lancaster.

From the later fourteenth century Pickering's story was one of rising repair and maintenance costs which failed to keep pace with the castle's evident decay. It played no active part in the Wars of the Roses, and by the outbreak of the Civil War in 1642 it was too far gone to be of use to either side; a survey of 1651 recorded that the chapel was the only roofed building left. Happily, the castle's down-at-heel and overgrown condition seems to have saved it from the extensive demolition which was certainly planned during the republican Commonwealth; and this most interesting motte-and-bailey development survived to be preserved in the present century.

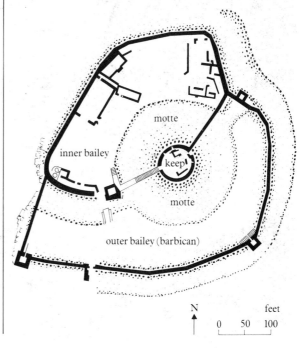

CLIFFORD'S TOWER, YORK

Department of the Environment

Clifford's Tower owes its name to Lord Robert Clifford, who was hanged in chains from the tower in 1322 after being captured by Edward II (one of the rare effective performances of that hapless monarch) after supporting the rebellion of Thomas, Earl of Lancaster. The tower is the keep of York Castle and should therefore be compared with the White Tower at London, for York was in medieval times – as it had been during the Roman occupation – the capital of the North. Just like the Tower of London, Clifford's Tower and its adjoining castle complex have served as royal fortress and palace, as a prison, and as a judicial and administrative centre. (As if to complete the comparison, York castle precincts even housed tame deer and a raven in the eighteenth century.) But there the parallels end, for

York Castle precincts, with Clifford's Tower at the centre, and the last remaining corner flanking tower and section of curtain wall to the right.

The North Country's most elegant shell keep : a thirteenth-century reconstruction on the original Norman motte.

the castles of London and York were otherwise entirely different. The Tower of London was a great keep, subsequently encased in concentric walls, while York's castle was a motte-and-bailey which never received concentric defences; and Clifford's Tower survives as one of the finest, most unorthodox shell keeps in the land.

After William I's original motte-and-bailey was restored during the crushing of the Northern Rebellion in 1069, York Castle was left with earthwork-and-palisade defences for over 170 years, until Henry III ordered its reconstruction in stone (1244). During the twelfth century, when nearly every other castle of similar importance at least began the conversion to stone defences, York was denied even the simplest of stone shell keeps. That no more ambitious defences were needed at York during these decades is a grim reminder of William's devastation of the North in 1069–70 and its long-lived effects. But it meant that the great Norman motte at York was never crowned with a simple cylindrical stone keep, as at Arundel or Windsor. Instead, York Castle's reconstruction in 1244–64 centred on a shell keep of an entirely novel

design, reflecting the new ideas that transformed castle defences in the thirteenth century.

The new keep was not cylindrical, but *quadrilobate* – formed by four interlocking circles with their centres at the points of a square. No other English castle – not even the south coastal 'cloverleafs' of Deal and Walmer built by Henry VIII 300 years later – has this quadrilobate plan. The result was a neat combination of the advantages of flanking towers with the capacious circular courtyard of more orthodox shell keeps.

Clifford's Tower was not enclosed by the new bailey defences built at the same time, but rather connected to them by a ramp and drawbridge. They consisted of a curtain wall with round towers, with water defences to the north side provided by the damming of the river Foss. This bailey wall survived the siege of York in the Civil War, of which the medieval city walls bore the brunt, but only the southern angle remains today. The rest was removed during the eighteenth and nineteenth centuries, when the bailey was developed as a judicial and penal centre, with Assize Courts, a female prison and a debtors' prison.

HELMSLEY, NORTH YORKSHIRE

Department of the Environment
A170 from Thirsk, Pickering

Helmsley is a good example of a castle at the transitional stage between tower keep and concentric plan. It is an unusually symmetrical keep-and-bailey castle of the late twelfth century, with a curtain wall and flanking corner towers, and a barbican and concentric outer banks and ditches added in the thirteenth century. The castle stood only one recorded siege, in the English Civil War, and paid for it with a thorough slighting which levelled the curtain wall and left only half the keep standing. But there is plenty still to see.

The castle stands on a table of rock which seems to have dictated the rectangular defence perimeter from the start; no trace of a motte has been found. Helmsley was originally granted by William I to Robert of Mortain, the noted castle-builder responsible for Pevensey, who almost certainly built some form of palisade and wooden hall on the site; but the oldest stone buildings were the work of Robert de Roos (1186–1227). Though it was destroyed in the slighting, the outer face of the keep was originally given a most unusual rounded shape, with the keep's inner walls angled to conform with the outer curve. Here we have a late tower keep designed to double as a round flanking tower – a sophisticated stage in the evolution of the 'keepless' concentric castle.

The grandson of Robert de Roos, of the same name, added nicely to the family fortunes by marrying Isabel Daubeny, the rich heiress of Belvoir in Leicestershire; and it is a reasonable assumption that he used the proceeds to transform

Helmsley Castle, showing the curtain wall, moat and levelled corner tower, with the half-destroyed keep in the background.

Helmsley's defences during his tenure of the castle (1258–85). Two fully-concentric ditches and banks were added, together with an unusually large barbican of which only the outer face and gatehouse have survived. No trace of masonry walls has been found on the outer banks, but they could well have been crowned with palisades. These additions were followed by the square west tower, from which were extended the sixteenth-century domestic apartments of the west range. Tracing the later buildings at Helmsley is made easier because they are of brown sandstone, standing out clearly against the white limestone of earlier work.

Helmsley has been in continuous ownership since

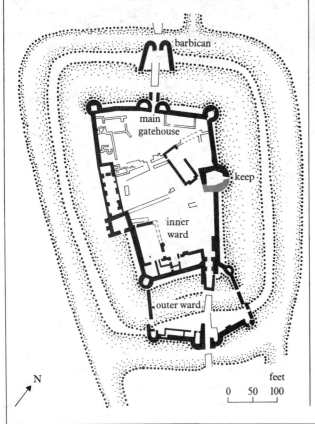

barbican

main gatehouse

keep

inner ward

outer ward

N

feet
0   50   100

*A besieger's-eye view of
Helmsley keep.*

its foundation, the present owners being the Earls of Feversham. The owner at the time of the English Civil War was the second Duke of Buckingham, but he was not in residence in 1644 when Sir Jordan Crosland defended Helmsley for Charles I against Sir Thomas Fairfax. When Crosland surrendered after a three-months' siege (November 1644) Fairfax levelled the curtain walls, barbican and inner keep. Ironically, when Buckingham returned to his ruined inheritance in 1657 he married Mary Fairfax – daughter of the man who had done all the damage 13 years before.

DURHAM

University of Durham

Durham Castle and the towering mass of the Norman Cathedral form the centrepiece of one of the most visually dramatic of all English cities. They stand on a high sandstone bluff ringed by a tight bend of the river Wear, and dominate the city from every viewpoint.

From the Norman Conquest of 1066 until 1836, the tight partnership of Durham Castle and Dur-

The imposing Tunstall Chapel: a reminder that Durham Castle was the palace as well as the stronghold of the prince-bishops of the Palatinate.

ham Cathedral symbolized a unique blend of Church and lay authorities. When Earl Waltheof was executed for treason by William I in 1074, the prince-bishops of the Palatinate of Durham took over the civil and military powers formerly wielded by the Old English earls, and before them the kings, of Northumbria. The powers of the bishops of Durham were unique: they were lay rulers as well as princes of the Church, and the Durham Palatinate

could mint its own coins, flaunt its own nobility in its own courts – even call out its own army. Durham Castle was, from its foundation, the bishop's palace as well as the key strongpoint of the city's defences.

The last Count Palatine of Durham, Bishop van Mildert, presented the castle to the new University of Durham in 1836, and it remains part of the University today. Because of this, visitors to Durham are best able to see the castle in the first three weeks of April and in the summer vacation – July to September – when the castle is open both morning and afternoon. For the rest of the year it is open only in the afternoon.

Durham Castle's old fighting ditch is now filled in, but apart from its many fine paintings and armour displays there is much to see, including the Norman crypt chapel, the late thirteenth-century Great Hall, and the splendid fifteenth-century kitchens.

Durham Castle's beautiful Norman chapel.

Arguably the most spectacular castle site in the whole of Britain: Durham Castle standing next to the Cathedral on its high sandstone bluff above the Wear.

BARNARD CASTLE, DURHAM

Department of the Environment
A67 from Darlington; A688 from Bishop Auckland;
A66/A67 from Penrith

Barnard Castle marks the old frontier between England and Scotland in the 1150s, when Northumbria, Cumbria and Westmorland were still under Scottish rule. It was built in about 1155 by Bernard de Bailleul on a dominant site on a low cliff above the river Tees. The Bailleuls or Balliols were a powerful Anglo-Scottish family with extensive lands in Galloway as well as northern England, and Barnard Castle was their English seat. This was the family which, having founded Balliol College at Oxford in 1263, provided John de Balliol as the puppet ruler whom Edward I unsuccessfully tried to establish as King of Scotland in the 1290s.

It is easy to see that in its heyday Barnard Castle compared favourably in size with other large northern castles such as Alnwick, Bamburgh and Dunstanburgh. The ruins cover no less than 6½ acres (2·6 hectares), and the castle is remarkable for having been screened by four baileys – another early, twelfth-century instance, like Ludlow and Richmond, of the move towards fully concentric castle defences. The splendid view from the fourteenth-century Round Tower helped to inspire Sir Walter Scott to write *Rokeby*. This was a staunchly Yorkist castle, which passed to Richard III on his marriage to Lady Anne Neville.

There is a treat in store for art lovers at Barnard Castle: another, much later 'castle', the Bowes Museum, a nineteenth-century imitation French château which houses one of the North Country's most famous collections of paintings, ceramics and furniture.

The twelfth-century curtain wall and square towers of Barnard Castle, with the later circular keep on the left.

The domestic face of Barnard Castle : the view across the fine surrounding countryside towards the chapel and great hall.

BROUGH, CUMBRIA

Department of the Environment
A66 from Penrith;
A67/A66 from Darlington via Barnard Castle

Brough is another very early Norman castle, like Peveril and Richmond, with a stone curtain wall dating from the late eleventh century. The castle is sited to command the upper reaches of Edendale, where the old Roman road (the modern A66) begins the long climb over Stainmore to the east. Brough's site makes it a 'hermit-crab' castle: the northern sector of the Roman fort of *Veterae*, built in the first century AD to keep the warrior tribesmen of the northern Brigantes penned in their hills.

The castle's development followed the standard pattern: an orthodox keep was added around 1175–1200, followed by a curtain wall with a prominent south-east round tower in the early reign of Henry III. As with Skipton, the excellent condition of Brough Castle today is due to the reconstruction ordered by Lady Anne Clifford, that remarkable and sadly unique castle-restorer of the late seventeenth century.

The impressive site of Brough Castle in Cumbria, commanding the upper reaches of Edendale.

The thirteenth-century round tower and curtain wall. Their deterioration was halted by the restoration work of Lady Anne Clifford after the English Civil War.

BROUGHAM, CUMBRIA

Department of the Environment
A66, 1½ miles (2·4 km) E of Penrith

Like Brough, the castle of Brougham occupies the
site of an important Roman fort, *Brocavum*, which
commanded the river crossing over the Eamont and
stood at the junction of two of the key Roman roads
piercing the Cumbrian hinterland. The outlines of
the Roman fort can still be seen outside the castle
walls.

A later castle than Brough by a century,
Brougham accordingly developed along different
lines: first the keep was built, around 1170–80, and
then the thirteenth-century curtain wall and towers.
Brougham was yet another castle of the Clifford
family, which held most of the former county of
Westmorland; but here the reconstruction achieved
by the indefatigable Lady Anne Clifford after the
Civil War was largely undone by her indigent
vandal of a grandson. He saw Brougham as a
convenient money-making stone quarry, and used it
accordingly.

*The view from Brougham Castle keep of the courtyard, the
thirteenth-century corner turret and surviving curtain wall,
and the outer ditch and bank.*

*The Eamont river crossing commanded by
Brougham Castle.*

CARLISLE, CUMBRIA

Borough of Carlisle

Carlisle was Roman *Luguvallium*, the western anchor of Hadrian's Wall against the Picts and Scots; and the town kept its role as a frontier bastion against Scottish invasions until the southward march of 'Bonnie Prince Charlie' in 1745. Like the other no-man's-land town of the Anglo-Scottish conflict, Berwick on the east coast, Carlisle was a frontier outpost which frequently passed from English to Scottish hands and back, whenever the Scots pressed their long-standing claim to the northern English counties of Northumbria, Cumbria, and Westmorland. Between the Norman Conquest of England in 1066 and the settlement of the Anglo-Scottish frontier in 1237, Carlisle changed hands no fewer than five times: Scottish until its conquest by William II in 1092; English until its seizure by David I of Scotland in 1035, profiting by the death of Henry I; recovered by Henry II in 1157; conquered again in 1216 when Alexander II of Scotland invaded the English North on behalf of Prince Louis of France; and recovered again, this time for good, when the English royalists triumphed and Prince Louis went home.

Given Carlisle's strategic importance – equal to Dover's, as the bastion of the north-west frontier at the other end of the country – one might expect to find a castle of exceptional size and strength there; but this is not the case. During the formative twelfth century, in which more southerly city castles like the Tower of London or Lincoln were steadily expanded, there was no unbroken continuity of occupation at Carlisle. Henry II added a keep to the castle begun on the north side of the town by William II in 1092, but the resulting combination was only embellished rather than transformed by Henry III and Edward I. Both these great castle-building kings concentrated on expensive priorities further south.

In a way, Carlisle Castle suffered architecturally from being in the wrong hands at the wrong time. When Edward I began his war to subdue Scotland in 1295, Carlisle was his western base camp – not a key enemy objective to be captured and made secure with a concentric giant castle like those he built in Wales. Nevertheless, the castle's fourteenth-century main gate has survived as a reminder of its stout defence after the English humiliation at Bannockburn in 1314, when the victorious Scots raided as far south as Richmond in Yorkshire.

Carlisle Castle always suffered from a common complaint of city castles: it was too hemmed in by the town, and so was an indifferent citadel. In 1540–3 Henry VIII ordered an entirely new citadel to be built in the town and it was this building, not the old castle, which was fully maintained and eventually reconstructed in 1807.

The fact remains that Carlisle Castle has seen more action than most English castles: in the medieval Scottish sieges of 1174, 1216 and 1314–18; in the Civil War siege of 1644–5, when it was attacked by the Presbyterian Scots fighting as Parliament's allies; it fell for the last time in its history to the Jacobites of Prince Charles Edward Stuart in 1745. Today, Carlisle Castle most appropriately houses the museum of the King's Own Border Regiment.

Stronghold against the Scots: the twelfth-century keep of Carlisle Castle, which over the centuries has seen more action than most other English castles.

NEWCASTLE-UPON-TYNE, NORTHUMBERLAND

Borough of Newcastle

The 'new castle' of Newcastle's name was the earthwork-and-timber fortification built under William I in 1080, to command the Tyne crossing at the eastern end of Hadrian's Wall. The enormous rectangular stone keep, with walls 16 feet (4·8 metres) thick, was built under Henry II in 1171–5. When completed in its new form it was the strongest fortress in the north – its equivalents in Henry II's castle-building programme being Nottingham in the Midlands, Orford in East Anglia and Dover on the Channel coast.

The deterrent effect of Henry II's new castle on the Tyne was immediately demonstrated during the Scottish invasion led by King William 'The Lion' in 1174. William considered Newcastle impregnable and left it strictly alone, confining his efforts to Carlisle and the weaker castles of the north. In the later thirteenth century Newcastle was Edward I's main base in the north-east for operations against Scotland. It was at Newcastle that Edward's chosen puppet-king of Scotland, John de Balliol – after swearing fealty at Norham and being enthroned at Scone – did homage to Edward for his new realm in December 1296.

The battlemented roof of the keep at Newcastle has been restored; it offers impressive if hardly beautiful views of the Tyne. As with Newcastle's western counterpart, Carlisle, the keep's outermost defences consisted of the town walls, built primarily to take the first shock of Scottish attacks. Newcastle's walls, part of which can still be seen in Bath Lane, were begun in 1280. When completed they were 2 miles (3·2 km) in circumference. At the same time, the keep's main entrance was given extra protection with the building of the Black Gate.

Both the keep and the Black Gate house museum collections today. That of the keep covers the castle's history from 1171; that of the Black Gate is a decided rarity, a bagpipe museum! Together they make this unusually complete town citadel of the twelfth and thirteenth centuries of special interest to visitors.

The restored battlements of the keep at Newcastle, built in the 1170s on Henry II's orders to be the strongest castle in the North Country.

ALNWICK, NORTHUMBERLAND

Privately owned
A1 or A189/A1068 from Newcastle; A1 from Berwick-upon-Tweed

Alnwick is the Arundel of the North Country. It is a triumph of nineteenth-century internal and external preservation and reconstruction, converting one of medieval England's most embattled castles into a princely residence. Alnwick is still the seat of the Dukes of Northumberland: the functioning heart of a great English estate. The dukedom is a comparatively recent one. It was conferred in 1766 on the husband of the latest female descendant of the family which had held Alnwick Castle since its great days in the fourteenth and fifteenth centuries: the Percys of Northumbria.

Alnwick's founders, and first owners until the male line died out in 1297, were the de Vesceys. The first of the castle's many moments of glory came about 35 years after its foundation in Stephen's reign: the capture of King William 'The Lion' of Scotland in 1174, which abruptly cut short a Scottish invasion that had already recoiled from Carlisle and turned east in hopes of easier prey. (The Scottish King was captured in a surprise attack, having incautiously ridden too close to the castle in foggy weather.) On the death of the last de Vescey in 1297, Alnwick was held in trust by the bishopric of Durham until its sale to Henry Percy in 1309. During the castle's first century in Percy hands, it was extensively rebuilt with a curtain wall, round towers and a barbican, becoming more or less the fighting shell that the visitor sees today.

Alnwick Castle's domination of its surroundings was enhanced by extensive landscape-gardening in the eighteenth and nineteenth centuries. One of the most impressive viewpoints is from the north, across the river Alne, with the castle looming starkly

Alnwick's barbican, with its battlements manned by decoy 'defenders' to encourage the waste of enemy arrows.

The superb view across the river Alne of the fighting profile of Alnwick Castle,
stronghold of the Percys.

One of the decoy garrison manning the barbican at Alnwick,
poised to hurl a rock on the heads of attackers.

against the sky – the profile which Alnwick presented to many generations of Scottish invaders and marauding bands of Douglases, blood enemies of the Percys. The entrance is on the south side, guarded by a fine barbican. The barbican is a distinct novelty because its battlements are 'guarded' by sentries of stone (most of them, admittedly, restored in the eighteenth century, but a few dating from the fourteenth). These statues were no mere decorative whim: they were decoy targets, to encourage besieging marksmen to waste their arrows. From the barbican a bridge leads over the moat (recently excavated) which once joined the Alne, and into the outer bailey.

There are many splendid attractions awaiting the visitor inside Alnwick – the enormous library, the Grand Staircase, the armoury in the Constable's Tower, and the fine museum of British and Roman antiquities housed in the Postern Tower. All are open to the public at advertised times – remember that this is a home, not a museum. Alnwick town makes a pleasant visit in its own right; anglers will not need reminding that this is where the famous Hardy fly rods come from. Altogether, Alnwick makes a splendid day out.

BAMBURGH, NORTHUMBERLAND

Privately owned
A1/B1342 from Berwick-upon-Tweed via Belford;
A1/B1341 from Newcastle via Alnwick and Adderstone

Bamburgh is one of the oldest sites in English history, being the earliest recorded stronghold built by the invading Anglo-Saxons in the sixth century AD. The *Anglo-Saxon Chronicle* records that King Ida of Bernicia (northernmost of the two sub-kingdoms which made up the later Anglo-Saxon kingdom of Northumbria) fortified the rock of Bamburgh in 547. The name derives from Bebba, queen of Ida's grandson Ethelfrith: *Bebbanburh*, or 'Bebba's Town'. In the ninth century, when North-umbria went down in ruin to the Great Army of the Danes, the last free Englishmen of the North held on at Bamburgh, with no English king left to whom they could give their allegiance but Alfred the Great in the south. Two hundred years later, therefore, the Normans inherited both a superb natural castle site and a fighting tradition second to none.

The present castle stands on the headland of Bamburgh, protected to seaward by a 150-foot (45.7-m) sheer precipice. In 1095 the first Norman

Bamburgh Castle from the foreshore, with a fine view of the rectangular keep added by Henry II in the later twelfth century.

Bamburgh Castle on its headland, commanding one of the oldest natural defensive sites in northern England.

castle held out against William II in the revolt by Robert de Mowbray, Earl of Northumberland, and proved impossible to take even when Earl Robert was captured. His wife continued to resist, and the siege dragged on. It was only ended by means of blackmail, Countess Matilda surrendering on the King's threat that her husband would be blinded if she did not. Once Henry II had added the rectangular keep in the following century, Bamburgh's strength remained unassailable until the advent of cannon in the fifteenth century.

Bamburgh featured prominently in the Wars of the Roses, as one of the strongest Percy castles in the North Country. After the first coronation of the Yorkist Edward IV in 1461, the refugee King Henry VI and his Queen Margaret began an attempted Lancastrian comeback by returning to Bamburgh with Scottish help. For nine months (autumn 1463– May 1464) the illusion of Lancastrian rule was maintained from behind Bamburgh's walls; and when Warwick 'The Kingmaker' led a Yorkist army to recover the Lancastrian castles of the North, Bamburgh was, true to tradition, the last to hold out. Warwick thereupon made an end with artillery, his gunners breaching the walls and enabling the castle to be taken by assault: the first time that the capture of an English castle had been preceded by a cannon bombardment.

None of the extensive reconstructions in the eighteenth and nineteenth centuries have managed to detract from the grandeur of Bamburgh, still one of the most impressive castles of the North Country: a defiant mass of red sandstone on its ancient headland.

One of the strongest of the North Country Percy castles, Bamburgh remained

virtually impregnable until the advent of cannon in the fifteenth century.

DUNSTANBURGH, NORTHUMBERLAND

Department of the Environment
1½ miles (2·4 km) N of Craster, 2 miles (3·2 km) ESE of Embleton;
buses to both villages from Alnwick

From whichever direction you approach, and however close you may manage to park, the only way to reach Dunstanburgh today is on foot. This makes it advisable to visit it in dry weather, because the shortest walk is well over a mile; but this is not a castle to miss. For at its full splendour in the mid-fifteenth century, before its ruinous downfall in the Wars of the Roses, Dunstanburgh was one of the biggest and most beautiful castles in all England, with a mighty sweep of curtain wall enclosing a defended area of 10 acres (4 hectares) in extent. Though Yorkist cannon and slighting parties reduced it to splintered pinnacles 500 years ago, the ruins of Dunstanburgh still proclaim the glory of castles before the age of cannon.

Unlike Alnwick and Bamburgh, its partners in the Northumbrian 'big three', Dunstanburgh was not an ancient fortified site, or even a development of an eleventh- or twelfth-century castle. It was begun in 1313 by Thomas, Earl of Lancaster, the first stage being a long moat to enclose the headland, and a tower gatehouse. The granting of a licence to wall and crenellate by Edward II in August 1316 seems to have been a royal attempt to save face, for by then the castle's curtain wall was already virtually complete.

One of the most interesting modifications to Dunstanburgh's original defences was made in 1380 by John of Gaunt, Duke of Lancaster. He ordered the conversion of the twin-tower gatehouse into a fully enclosed keep. An inner square tower, connected to the outer curtain, was built behind the eastern gatehouse tower; and a new entrance was made outside this newly-created inner ward, screened by

An aerial view of Dunstanburgh from the north-east, showing the enormous circuit of the curtain wall and the massive keep at the right centre.

Dunstanburgh's north-eastern flank was guarded by the square Lilburn Tower, a postern gate for unleashing counter-attacks against besiegers.

a long barbican. Ingenious though it was, however, this reconstruction did little more than re-state the old obsession with converting the castle's weakest point (the main gateway) into its strongest point (the tower gatehouse). Neither Gaunt nor his successors added platforms or ports for the mounting of defensive artillery, without which enemy siege guns could be brought up with impunity to batter the walls at close range. This preoccupation with outdated techniques spelled Dunstanburgh's ruin during the repeated Yorkist sieges in 1462–4.

A series of Tudor surveys assessing the cost of repairing Dunstanburgh throughout the sixteenth century indicate that the keep, large stretches of the curtain wall, and the flanking towers remained in surprisingly good repair until about 1580, by which time the timbers of the roofs and floors had gone. In 1603, however, James VI of Scotland became James I of England, and Dunstanburgh lost its original role as a barrier against Scottish invasions. The unsupported stonework was left to degenerate into the splendid ruins the visitor sees today. There was no conceivable role for Dunstanburgh as a coastal-defence fortress; like Scarborough, it stood with its back to the sea. Dunstanburgh's real problem, however, was that it also faced back towards the past.

Battered by five centuries of North Sea gales: the weathered stones of Dunstanburgh, with arrow-slit and garderobe shoot.

WARKWORTH, NORTHUMBERLAND

Department of the Environment
A1068 from Alnwick;
A1068 from Newcastle via Newbiggin-by-the-Sea

Lying only 6 miles (9·6 km) south-east of Alnwick, Warkworth is, predictably, another of the great Percy castles of the North Country. In many ways, it is a more impressive castle than Alnwick, for it is the North Country's finest specimen of a 'growth' castle, carrying the stamp of consistent development from the eleventh to the fourteenth centuries.

Warkworth is also that considerable rarity, a castle with a fourteenth-century great tower on an earth motte, as at Dudley and York.

The first castle built at Warkworth, in a bend of the river Coquet, may have been of late eleventh-century vintage, but a motte-and-bailey was certainly established there by 1139. It escaped the

The Coquet river at Warkworth, commanded by the great tower residence of the Percys – one of the very few great towers built on an earlier motte.

destruction of adulterine (unlicensed) castles of similar date early in the reign of Henry II, and a rectangular curtain wall was added in the following century. The real transformation, however, was wrought under Percy management in the late fourteenth and early fifteenth centuries: the building of the great tower on the motte. This is of a plan unique in England, that of a 'Greek cross': a square tower with projecting flanking towers formed by the arms of a cross. Warkworth's tower is, however, nothing like the solid mass of Clifford's Tower at York: it was unmistakably built for residential comfort just as much as for defensibility, with a lavish allocation of windows.

The tower escaped the worst damage inflicted by repeated sieges, of which it endured two in the English Civil War – by the Scots in the Marston Moor campaign of 1644 and by the Parliamentarians in 1648, who slighted it when they withdrew. In 1672, Warkworth's bailey defences suffered their worst-ever damage when the castle was 'cannibalized' for building materials; but the great tower still stands proudly on its motte, one of the most prized ornaments of the Percy family for nearly 500 years.

Family residence as well as fighting stronghold : the chapel at Warkworth, looking towards the altar.

The unique feature of Warkworth Castle is its great tower, completed in the early fifteenth century in the shape of a Greek cross.

NORHAM, NORTHUMBERLAND

Department of the Environment
A698/B6470 from Berwick-upon-Tweed

The road from Berwick, 8 miles (12·9 km) to the north-east, runs through the filled-in moat of what was once one of the strongest border fortresses in England. This magnificent rectangular keep (90 ft high × 84 ft × 60 ft/27·4 × 25·6 × 18·3 m) was built in the 1160s to safeguard the three northern counties after their recovery by Henry II from Scottish rule. Norham was not, however, a royal castle (though it often reverted to royal control in succeeding centuries). It was built by the formidable Hugh de Puiset, Bishop of Durham, and should be seen as a symbol of the raw power wielded by the prince-bishops of the Durham palatinate. Bishop Hugh's splendid keep was a massive replacement for the earlier castle built at Norham in Stephen's reign (1121) and destroyed by the Scots.

The new castle's first adventure came in 1173–4, when Bishop Hugh, collaborating with the very menace which Norham had been built to check – a Scottish invasion – joined the rebellion against Henry II. When this ended so unexpectedly with the surprise capture of William 'the Lion' under the walls of Alnwick (*see* p. 136) the discomfited Bishop was obliged to surrender Norham to the King with his other castles. It was at Norham, in November 1292, that John de Balliol swore fealty to Edward I as vassal King of Scotland, before his temporary instalment on the Scottish throne – the first step, for the English, on the road to their defeat at Bannockburn 22 years later. In the Wars of the Roses, Norham surrendered to Warwick's army after the fall of Alnwick, thus preserving largely intact one of the finest and most imposing of England's many twelfth-century 'great keeps'.

Broad-backed twelfth-century vaulting supports the mass of the keep.

The huge keep of Norham Castle, built after 1160 to secure the northern counties after their recovery from Scottish rule.

OTHER CASTLES TO VISIT

Knaresborough, South Yorkshire
Keep, fourteenth-century gatehouse, curtain wall and towers added to original Norman foundations. Museum contains armour worn at Marston Moor in Civil War.

Middleham, North Yorkshire
Fine keep of late twelfth century, though outer curtain demolished and ditch filled in.

Muncaster, Cumbria
Privately-owned nineteenth-century reconstructed mansion (by Anthony Salvin) incorporating twelfth-century square tower.

Sizergh, Cumbria
Fourteenth-century peel tower with Tudor Great Hall; further seventeenth- and eighteenth-century additions.

Lumley, Durham
Fourteenth-century fortified manor, with palatial eighteenth-century reconstruction by Vanbrugh. Today a luxury hotel noted for 'medieval banquets'.

Raby, Durham
Famous Neville stronghold of fourteenth and fifteenth centuries, with nine distinctive towers. Still superb despite removal of outer curtain walls and draining of moat.

GLOSSARY

adulterine castles Unlicensed castles, built without Crown permission during the prolonged civil wars or 'Anarchy' of King Stephen's reign (1135–54). Most were pulled down by his successor Henry II (1154–89).

bailey Enclosed area screening castle's main defences.

barbican Outer tower or walled area blocking direct approach to main gate of castle.

bastion Platform or low tower projecting from main walls to increase effective defensive fire. Originally of rounded shape; usually pointed from 1540s on.

battering Sloping a wall inward from a wider base for greater strength.

concentric castles Castles with two or more lines of defence, one inside the other with the innermost higher than the outer, creating a web studded with mutually supporting strongpoints.

crenellations, crenellate Fighting battlements consisting of stone *merlons* interspersed with *embrasures* which permitted defensive fire. 'Licence to crenellate' was the Crown's permission to fortify an existing manor house or build a new castle.

curtain wall Perimeter wall surrounding *bailey* or *keep*. Usually studded with *flanking towers*.

donjon Medieval name for *keep*; originally the wooden tower built on the *motte*.

drawbridge Wooden bridge across ditch or *moat*, raised to complete circuit of outer defences and prevent direct attack on gate. Would be raised at night.

embrasure Gap between *merlons* to permit defensive fire (archery or other missiles) against attackers below.

enceinte Fortified enclosure, usually referring to circuit of outer ramparts with bastions for the emplacing of guns.

flanking towers Towers projecting from corners of *keep* or main stretch of *curtain wall*, both to strengthen the structure and bring foot of wall under defensive fire.

garderobe Latrine.

gatehouse Defences protecting main castle entrance, often the strongest point of the castle.

hoard *also* **brattice** Wooden platform rigged outside battlements to allow missiles to be dropped on attackers below. From fourteenth century, supplanted by permanent stone *machicolation*.

keep Later word for *donjon*: the castle's stronghold, usually a tower.

linear castles Castles with *baileys* or *wards* arranged in a chain, instead of one inside the other as with *concentric castles*. The usual development of castles sited on ridges of high ground.

machicolation Stone platform extending out from top of battlements, supported on small arches; fulfilled role of earlier wooden *hoards*.

merlon Stone section of battlements, interspersed by *embrasures*. Often pierced for additional defensive fire.

mine Tunnel driven by besiegers under castle defences, to bring down a tower, corner of *keep*, or key stretch of wall in order to create a breach for a decisive assault.

moat Water-filled ditch, often linked to nearby river or stream.

motte Shaped natural hill, or wholly artificial mound, on which *donjon* was built. Strongpoint of early castle defences.

murder hole (also *meurtrière*) Opening in *gatehouse* porch ceiling and/or wall to allow attackers, trying to force gate or *portcullis*, to be attacked without means of retaliation.

peel or **pele tower** Tower stronghold without outer defences, for defence against Border raids.

portcullis Heavy wooden gate shod with iron, mounted in grooves, which could be dropped to block a key gateway or passage. Attackers thus trapped could then be attacked through *murder holes*.

slighted Deliberately rendered indefensible by being wholly or partly demolished.

solar Upper-storey private room offering privacy to lord and family. Often accessible only by outside staircase.

ward Enclosed defensive area; later word for *bailey*.

FURTHER READING

Allen Brown, R., *English Medieval Castles* (Batsford, 1954)
Cormack, Patrick, *Castles of Britain* (Artus, 1982)
Hindley, G., *Castles of Europe* (Hamlyn, 1968)
Turner, H. L., *Town Defences in England and Wales* (John Baker, 1971)

Warner, Philip, *The Medieval Castle* (Arthur Barker, 1971); *A Guide to Castles in Britain* (New English Library, 1976)
Wise, Terence, *Forts and Castles* (Almark, 1972); *Medieval Warfare* (Osprey, 1976)

ACKNOWLEDGMENTS

Photographs are reproduced by kind permission of the following:

Aerofilms Ltd: 10 left and right, 13, 18, 32, 36, 52, 54, 55, 77, 78, 119 top, 125, 145 bottom
James Austin: 86 left and right
John Bethell: 15, 22, 44 left and right, 45, 47, 49, 57 top, 58, 59 top, 62, 63, 64 left, 65, 80, 82, 85, 94, 96 top and bottom, 97 top and bottom, 103, 107 top and bottom, 112–3, 124, 132 bottom, 133 bottom, 140–1
Bodleian Library: 119 bottom
Janet and Colin Bord: 108 right, 110 left, 111 top and bottom
British Tourist Authority: 105
Cambridge University Aerial Survey: 25, 142
Peter Chèze-Brown: endpapers, opp. title page, 11, 12 left, 20, 21, 23, 30, 31 bottom, 35, 39 bottom, 68, 69 bottom, 71, 72 left, 73 top and bottom, 74 left and right, 76 top and bottom, 90, 91 bottom, 98 left, 99, 120, 129, 132 top, 133 top, 137 top, 139, 143 bottom, 146, 147
Fotobank/ETB: 60, 87 bottom, 121, 127, 131, 135, 136, 137 bottom
Michael Holford: 9 (Ianthe Ruthven), 14, 31 top, 34, 61, 67 (Ethel Hurwicz), 88–9, 91 top

Angelo Hornak: 26
Jarrolds, Norwich: 66 top, 106
A. F. Kersting: 33 left, 39 top, 59 bottom, 66 bottom, 70, 75, 81, 95, 102, 104, 114, 116, 123 left, 130, 134, 143 top, 144, 145 top
Lithograve (Birmingham) Ltd: 100
S. & O. Mathews: 17, 43 top
National Trust: 12 right, 40 left and right
Walter Scott, Bradford: 126 right
Kenneth Scowen: 28 top, 33 right, 37, 38 right, 41 top, 42 left, 42 right, 56 left, 79
Edwin Smith: 41 bottom, 53 top and bottom, 93, 101 left and right, 108 left
Tate Gallery: 84
Derek Widdicombe: copyright page, 19, 57 bottom, 117, 118, 122, 128 left and right, 138
Andy Williams: 50–1
Trevor Wood: 83, 86 left, 92 left and right, 109
Woodmansterne Ltd: 43 bottom (Clive Friend FIIP), 48 (Nicholas Servian FIIP)
Weidenfeld and Nicolson Archives: 27, 28 bottom, 29

Castle plans by Line and Line

INDEX